MW00395595

The John Project

A Devotional Commentary

Volume One

Randy Boldt

All Scripture quotes are taken from the New King James Version®. Copyright © 1982 by Thomas Nelson. Used by permission. All rights reserved.

Copyright © 2019 Randy Boldt
All rights reserved.
ISBN-13: 978-1-7945-6856-3

DEDICATION

To Sue Boldt, my beautiful bride.

Your luminous life stirs my soul with such passion and my spirit with such humble gratitude to God that I can't even begin to express my heart. But this I know as surely as anything in this world: I love you with every fiber of my being and I cannot conceive of a life worth living without you in it.

CONTENTS

FOREWORD

I've known Randy Boldt for a very long time – since he was in his teens and I was less than a year into pastoring the first Hope Chapel.

Randy led one of the hottest bands in Southern California during the Jesus Movement of the 1970s. We had the privilege of them deciding to join our church. They shaped our music but more than that they helped shape our thinking.

Randy wrote most of the lyrics to the songs they sang, impressing me with a deep grasp of Scripture – the kind you only get from loving it. These were rock songs that reflected the insights of the great hymn-writers of the past. Randy Boldt was and is a man of the word.

Our friendship spans decades during which I've watched Randy and Sue plant and lead several fruitful congregations. They are some of my heroes.

And then this book comes along...

I watched a couple of the videos that led up to this devotional guide, but I'm not much into videos so they barely caught my attention. However, that all changed once I got a copy of the distilled version you hold in your hands. You see, I get bored reading Scripture. This is the downside of teaching it several times a week over a long period of time. What I found in *The John Project* is living water, sweet and satisfying to a person looking for fresh insights into the God I love.

The book offers bite-size chunks of deep truth. You'll find yourself hungry for more. My advice: read only one devotional each day (it's hard to stop with just one) and then meditate on what you read. Like me, you'll find renewed sustenance in Jesus.

Ralph Moore

Ralph Moore is the founding pastor of the Hope Chapel movement now numbering over 2,300 churches worldwide. He currently serves as the Multiplication Catalyst for Exponential.org.

INTRODUCTION

It was an Accident

One day, I sensed the Lord nudging me to shake up my devotional reading. For decades, I'd used a daily plan that allowed me to read through the Bible each year. I call it *reading for distance*. Although I was determined to continue doing that, I now felt Jesus inviting me to also *read for depth*, and not just for sermon preparation. It was about focusing on one small chunk of Scripture at a time and allowing the Holy Spirit to speak to me through it.

I randomly decided to start with the Gospel of John and take it slow – savoring a verse or two or three over a period of at least a whole day – letting the Lord saturate my life with it.

I started with chapter one, verse one. And as I was meditating on it, I decided to step outside my office and go for a short walk. As I did, I started talking out loud to myself about the verse. I found that process opened things up for me in a powerful way.

I wanted to document what I was experiencing so I wouldn't forget it. So, I reached into my pocket, grabbed my phone, and started videoing myself as I verbally considered what the Lord was teaching me through the passage. Afterward, I decided to share that short video on social media. I received several comments from friends who said it had been helpful to them. So, I kept up this simple process, creating a video chronicle of my journey through John.

That's how I accidentally began to record a devotional video commentary. (All the video and audio files are available at randyboldt.com/john.)

As time passed, I learned to look into the camera lens and a few other things that helped improve the video quality. I also changed the process a bit by scripting my thoughts before recording them. So, the content became more focused and refined along the way.

When I completed the first six chapters after nearly 100 episodes, I decided to try and create a short book containing the commentaries I'd finished so far.

I transcribed the videos that hadn't been scripted, edited everything so that it would make sense without the visuals, and this is the result. I primarily wanted to chronicle my own journey of discovery, but I humbly submit it for your consideration as well.

Here's what I hope you'll glean from the experience:

- That by taking a road trip through an entire book of the Bible at a pace that allows time to not only stop and smell the roses but consider the one who planted them and for what purpose, you'll discover the value and adopt the practice of interacting with the Bible in a more holistic way. Instead of thinking of Scripture as a collection of blossoms to pick through randomly, I desire to entice you with the pleasure of a stroll through an entire field of blooms.
- That by engaging with God's word consistently you'll develop a craving for its delicacies along with the holy habit of regularly exposing your soul to its life-giving

nourishment.

- That by reading the words the Holy Spirit breathed onto the pages of John's Gospel, you'll learn how to hear the ones he whispers to your heart.

I've quoted a bit of the Scripture covered at the beginning of each section. But my desire is that whether you read this as an inspirational book, a daily devotional, or a reference source, you'll open your own Bible (or Bible app) and read the whole text alongside it. What I've written is only meant to serve as a catalyst for your personal interaction with the word of God.

Will there be a Volume Two? I hope so. This has been a deeply rewarding experience. So, I've decided to keep at it for my own benefit and perhaps yours too.

CHAPTER ONE

1:1 • Eternal Communicator

In the beginning was the word, and the word was with God, and the word was God.

John 1:1

No one can know for certain why the Holy Spirit moved John to open his Gospel by describing Jesus – God the Son – as the word. But it seems to me it had to have been at least in part to point us back to some of the very first concepts in the Bible. The opening phrase in the book of Genesis is, "In the beginning, God created..." Then, three sentences later, we're told that God created by speaking.

In the beginning...God said...

In the beginning was the word...

It seems to me the Spirit wants us to understand that Jesus is not a silent bystander or a voiceless observer on the scene of this world. He's an eternal communicator.

So, if Jesus is an eternal communicator, doesn't that mean he's speaking right now? And if he's speaking right now, shouldn't we take the time to listen?

Obviously, the answer to both questions is, yes. But if we're going to hear and act on what he's saying, we need to learn how he communicates with us. And thankfully, God hasn't left us in the dark. The Bible tells us at least three things to help our hearts become better sensitized to the sound of his voice.

Two of these clues are found in 1 Kings 19:11-12 where Elijah gets a lesson in hearing God. He learns that God's voice is *still* and *small*.

The word *still* in this passage means quiet. But that doesn't mean the Lord is speaking so as not to be heard. It means he's not going to compete for our attention. So, if we really want to hear him, we're going to have to work at turning down the volume of the white noise, ambient sound, and competing voices the devil uses to distract us.

The word *small* means compressed. And this means that instead of speaking in linear sentences where one word follows another like we do, there is so much God wants to say, he compresses it into packages that will take time and contemplation to unwrap. We need to learn to listen for packets not paragraphs.

The third clue is found in Isaiah 30:21 where it says God's instructions often sound like they're sneaking up on us from behind. This means what he says is frequently not what we expect. It's *surprising*. So, if we're going to improve our discernment, we need to pay more attention to those unexpected promptings from the Spirit.

My wife and I have been married for 45 years. Over that time, I've developed a keen sensitivity to her voice. I'd know it anywhere. I can pick it out of the noise of any crowd. And it's my deepest desire to get to know God's voice like that.

Because you've decided to read this book, I'll bet you desire the same thing. So, let's start listening more closely for his *still*, *small*, and *surprising* voice.

1:2 • Limitless

He was in the beginning with God.
John 1:2

At the point when everything else began, Jesus – God the Son – already was. The Bible is clear about that. Jesus is eternal. He has always been and forever will be. And everything he is continually flows into eternity from eternity. He is *infinite*. He is *limitless*. And those words describe a concept my intellect fails to grasp. But thinking about a river – although an imperfect illustration – helps.

The Napa River is not infinite. It has a starting point on the slopes of Mount Saint Helena, winds its way south, and empties into San Pablo Bay. Still, when I lived along its banks, I never asked myself, "What if it wasn't here? What if it ran dry? What if there wasn't enough water up there on Saint Helena and at some point, it just turned into a big, dry gulch?"

I never thought that way. Those things never crossed my mind. I imagined that its water was always going to flow from north to south.

So, when it comes to my Savior, why do I sometimes wonder, "Is he substantial enough? Does he have enough grace? Does he have enough love? Does he have enough patience? Does he have enough comfort? Are there enough material resources at his disposal to meet my needs?"

Why is that? Why do I think that way?

I'm not sure, but I know this: I don't want those questions to continue to be part of the way I think about God, about my Savior. Because this verse in John's Gospel tells me he has always been, and he always will be. There is no limit to anything about him.

So today, if you're concerned there might not be enough in the resources of our God, I ask you to reconsider that. Let's trust him today with all our needs.

1:3 • Creative Genius

All things were made through Him, and without Him nothing was made that was made.

John 1:3

Jesus was the creative genius, the architect, the designer, the engineer, the artist, the agent behind every good thing in this world. So why is it then, that when it comes to the major projects of our lives, we often don't even consult him?

Why is it that when we're building our relationships, marriages, families, careers, financial portfolios, etc. we feel like we have to do it alone? Is it because we think God is disinterested? Maybe it's just our foul pride that convinces us we know what we're doing and don't need his help.

Or maybe it isn't that at all. Maybe we just don't trust him to do a good enough job.

Oh! I pray that's not the case. But either way, I think we would be wise to pay closer attention to the promise of his trustworthiness embedded in this verse.

1:4 • The Real Thing

In Him was life, and the life was the light of men.
John 1:4

That word, *life,* is translated from the Greek word *zoe,* which the New Testament uses to describe the kind of life God has. It's not the word *bios,* which is used for biological life. It's not simply the kind of life produced by your heart beating in your chest and your blood pumping through your veins. This verse tells us the kind of life Jesus has to offer is something altogether different – a life of another kind – and that this life is what truly lights a person up.

I'm sure you're familiar with the word *nightlife.* It describes a nighttime party atmosphere where folks are drinking, dancing, enjoying music, and other entertainments. And for many people, it also describes an aspiration, a highlight, something they look forward to. It's even one of the measures used to rank the livability of cities. Our culture will say a city is a good place to live because it has great nightlife.

But seriously. Are we willing to settle for that – nightlife? Is lubricating your inhibitions with alcohol or some other intoxicant and moving your body to the beat of the music in the dim light of a club enough for you? Artificial life under artificial lights?

Not me. Not when the Lord is offering *zoe* – a life that's incomparably higher, greater, and deeper in every way. A life that's spiritual, eternal, substantial, fulfilling, exhilarating and so much more than words can describe.

Let's reject cheap knockoffs and choose to settle for nothing less than the real thing – the life we were made for, the life Jesus said would light us up.

1:5 • The Son is Rising

The light shines in the darkness, and the darkness did not comprehend it.
John 1:5

The word *comprehend* in this verse doesn't mean understand, as in the darkness doesn't understand the light. It means it can't lay hold of it, can't grasp it, can't extinguish it.

I stepped outside this morning to watch the sunrise. And the darkness that enshrouded the spot where I was standing just minutes before the sun came up gave way to the light. There wasn't a thing it could do about it. The light wins every time. In John 8:12 and again in 9:5, Jesus says that he is the Light of the World. And that means wherever he is, darkness can't remain.

I've been alive for over 60 years, and I don't recall a time in those many years that seemed as dark as the days we're living in right now. It seems like the news is bad everywhere. The natural world seems to be falling apart. The political world is in chaos. Violence is everywhere along with terrorism, wars, and on and on. And this is true not only of the larger world, but of our small world, our micro-world, your world. Things can seem pretty dark at times, can't they? And you can despair. You can start to wonder, "Where's the hope?"

But we have this amazing promise. "The darkness did not comprehend it." It can't do anything about the light of Jesus.

Let him shine in your corner of the world today. Let his light be on display in your life — what you say and what you do. And watch what happens. The Son is rising!

1:6-9 • A Sent One

There was a man sent from God, whose name was John.
John 1:6

These verses introduce us to John the Baptist and what he was sent to do – bear witness to the Light as a testimony of Jesus Christ in this world. But he was not the only person who has been sent by God. In fact, Jesus made it crystal clear that all his followers have been sent by him in exactly the same way to do exactly the same thing – bear testimony to the good news of Jesus (John 20:21).

And you know what? That means there's a woman sent by God whose name is Sally. There's a teenager sent by God whose name is Robert. There's a grandfather sent by God whose name is Joe. All of us – all of us who call Jesus, Lord – have been sent by him.

When I walked into my local Starbucks this morning, I wasn't just another customer – although I did buy a drink before I left. I went in there as one sent by God. Everywhere you and I go, we have been sent by God. We are people on assignment from heaven. We're not just moving through the routine of our day. We are people sent by God. Every door you walk through today, you enter that place as a person sent by God.

And that perspective changes the way you see things. It changes the way you think about how you're living, doesn't it? And that's a good thing.

You are a sent one.

1:10-11 • The Knock at the Door

He was in the world, and the world was made through Him, and the world did not know Him. He came to His own, and His own did not receive Him.
John 1:10-11

I mean, really. How is that even possible, that the God who made all things and who is present with us by his own declaration could be unknown to us? How is it that we miss him?

Could it be the reason we're so often unaware of or not experiencing the presence of God in our lives is that we simply fail to welcome him – we don't *receive* him?

Have you noticed that it's easy to miss things you're not looking for? In Revelation 3:20, Jesus says, "I stand at the door and knock." Maybe we're so busy with all the stuff of life, that we just fail to hear it. Perhaps we lose our sense of expectancy regarding his desire to show up in the midst of our routine and we carry on with our day leaving the Lord standing on the front porch, so to speak. And if that's the case, something needs to change.

Let's be listening for the knock at the door.

1:12 • A Heavenly Father

But as many as received Him, to them He gave the right to become
children of God, to those who believe in His name:
John 1:12

Forty-five years ago, Sue and I stood before our friends and
family in a church building. And there, before God, we
pledged our love to one another on our wedding day. I looked
into Sue's eyes and said, "I *receive* you as my wedded wife." I
didn't say, "I *believe* in you," but I did say, "I *commit* to you,"
which is really the sense of the word *believe* in this verse.

And on the basis of that *receiving* and *committing* to one
another, a relationship was born that we'd never had before.
After that day, I was able to refer to my girlfriend as my wife.
Sue was now my wife. But that was hard to say at first. It was
difficult to get those words out of my mouth. I almost choked
on them every time because it just seemed so incredible that I
was now married to this person. She was my wife!

It's even more challenging sometimes for me to refer to the
maker of all things as my Heavenly Father. The fact that I can
now rightfully consider myself a child of God simply because I
have *received* Jesus and *committed* myself to him is nearly
overwhelming.

It seems so presumptuous. It seems so unbelievable. But it's
true. And if you have given your heart to Jesus – *received* him as
your Lord and Savior and *committed* yourself to him in faith –
you have a Heavenly Father too.

1:13 • You in Mind

...who were born, not of blood, nor of the will of the flesh, nor of the will of man, but of God.
John 1:13

This verse is referring to those of us who have been born again and clarifies that this is not something we engineer by our flesh. It's not something we can make happen by force of will or anything else. It's because of God. God saved me. God saved you. God is the one who drew us to himself and caused us to become his children.

When you go to the drug store to buy toothpaste, before leaving you'll have to run the gauntlet of the impulse-buy items that are near the cash registers – gum, candy bars, lip balm, magazines. This is the stuff they know you didn't come in to buy. But they also know that while you're in line waiting to pay for your intended purchase, you might throw some of those other items into your basket as well and they've increased their sales.

Some of us think that God picked us up as an impulse-buy. He wasn't really seeking us. Jesus came to save the pretty ones, the smart ones, the spiritual ones, the ones that are better leaders, and that kind of thing. But somehow, we got picked up along with them almost accidentally. We're deeply grateful. But we don't imagine God was purposely after us.

But nothing could be further from the truth. It's cliché to say because it's such an overused phrase, but it's nonetheless true. When Jesus went to the cross, he had you in mind. And were you the only one – the only sinner, who needed his saving grace – he would have paid exactly the same price.

Let's live in the peace of that realization today and pause to thank him for his boundless love right now.

1:14 • Grace and Truth

And the word became flesh and dwelt among us, and we beheld His glory…full of grace and truth.
John 1:14

The other day, I brought my grandson to a little neighborhood park. Together, we climbed the stairs to the top of a gazebo, and he asked me, "Papa, what's a gazebo?" He'd never heard that word before. So, I said, "Well, a hundred years ago, people used to come to this little park to listen to music being performed and speeches given from up here. It made it possible for people down below to see and hear whoever was speaking, playing, or performing."

But in that park, the gazebo isn't used for that purpose anymore. It's really just for visitors to climb as we did and get a little different perspective on things, a little higher elevation, a little different altitude. And I like that. I like to just get a little different viewpoint from time to time.

And that reminds me of John 1:14 because it says that the word – Jesus, who became flesh and put God's glory or beauty on display among us – displayed that beauty in at least two ways: grace and truth.

I think all of us would agree that the grace of God displayed in Jesus is truly beautiful, stunning. The unmerited favor that those of us who have received Christ as our Savior have experienced is beyond description.

But God's truth is also amazingly gorgeous, breathtaking. And I mean even when he tells us the truth we don't want to hear, the things we need to see about ourselves from a different perspective, and the things that we need to change in our lives that no one else will tell us about.

I don't express my gratitude or thankfulness enough for the

gift of God's truth to me. But I want to join with you in praising God today for the beauty of his grace *and* truth. Let's watch and listen closely for *both*.

1:15 • He is First

John bore witness of Him and cried out, saying, "This was He of whom I said, 'He who comes after me is preferred before me, for He was before me.'"
John 1:15

This verse tells us John's testimony to the world was that Jesus comes first.

A few years ago, I was watching a long line of cars waiting to get off the island where I lived at the time and onto westbound California Highway 37. I'm fairly sure they weren't thinking, "Oh, I'm so glad I'm not first in line!" I know that's not how I would have felt. Any time I have to wait – any time I'm second – it bothers me. Maybe you too.

So, it makes me wonder about the testimony of my life. What do people hear my life declaring about Jesus? Is it that Jesus comes first or is it something else?

I want to live in a way that declares Jesus is first in my life. And I don't want to fake it. I want it to be the truth. In everything I think and do, every consideration, every plan, every interaction, every desire, I want him to be number one.

Do you feel the same? May this be our testimony today: Jesus is first.

1:16 • You Have it All

And of His fullness we have all received, and grace for grace.
John 1:16

One day, I was sitting in the airport waiting for my flight. I was trying to get on the internet to do some work and became so frustrated with how slow it was I finally just gave up. And as I was sitting there thinking about how frustrated I was, I realized I shouldn't really complain. There were so many people trying to get on the internet at the same time, of course the bandwidth was going to have to be spread thinly across all of the users.

But then, I realized I often think of my relationship with Jesus like that. I imagine there are so many people vying for his attention that his ability to focus on me must be diminished in some way because there is only so much of him to go around.

Theologically, I know better. But practically, sometimes I expect I'm just getting part of his fullness – part of his attention. However, this verse says just the opposite. It says, "…of his *fullness* we have all received." Everything he is and everything he has is always, at all times, ours.

And if that weren't enough, it says we've received, "grace for grace." Just about the time you are overcome by the realization of one aspect of his grace, here comes another.

That's the God we have. That's the Savior we have.

Today, if there's any reason you may be wondering how much of the Savior's attention you have, you have it all. You have it all.

1:17 • Don't Step Backward

For the law was given through Moses, but grace and truth came through Jesus Christ.
John 1:17

This isn't describing something that was bad and then was replaced by something good. It's talking about a progression in how God wants for us to experience him.

Law is all about simple obedience, and it's a good thing. God has made clear through the Mosaic law, Ten Commandments, and other instructions God gave his people in the Old Testament what is right and what is wrong. And we need that. But it doesn't require any relationship. It just requires obedience.

The problem is that none of us can fully keep the law. So, something has to change. And the Lord wants us to move from law-keeping and law-failing to grace and truth, which require relationship with the one who fulfilled the law for us.

When we stop relating to God through a list of do's and don'ts, we can begin to experience him as a Heavenly Father who covers us through his Son with unmerited favor and instructs us in his ways, guides us, and shapes us with his truth. And then, we're getting to where God wants us to be.

Don't step backward today. Don't relate to God as though he were a do-and-don't-do authoritarian lawgiver. Experience him as the one who fulfilled the law for you and offers you grace and truth.

1:18 • A Face on Himself

No one has seen God at any time. The only begotten Son…has declared Him.
John1:18

I recently walked by a building near my home and noticed a sign a film crew had painted on it to make it look like a high school gymnasium for a television show that was being filmed there. And that works fine for Hollywood. You paint a face on something and pretend that it is whatever you want it to be.

But that doesn't work so well when it comes to God. Still, a lot of us – including me – often do it even though the second of the Ten Commandments tells us not to. It says, "Don't make a carved image of God." Don't try to shape an image of what God is like based on your own preferences – what he should be or what he should do according to your desires. When we do, all we end up with are depictions of a god who is less than the real God.

But the great thing is, we don't have to do that. We don't have to paint a face on God. God literally revealed himself – put a face on himself – through Jesus. Open the Bible. Read Matthew, Mark, Luke, and John. Watch Jesus put God on display, the real God in the full spectrum of who he is: his power, his glory, his wisdom, his love, his patience.

And when you see God for who he is, you no longer want the flimsy knockoff of your imagination. And that's a good thing. That's a really, really good thing.

1:19-23 • Who We Are

Then they said to him, "Who are you, that we may give an answer to those who sent us? What do you say about yourself?" He said: "I am 'The voice of one crying in the wilderness: "Make straight the way of the Lord...""

John 1:22-23a

The prologue has concluded, and now we're moving into the narrative section of the Gospel. And as we do, I want to ask you something. Have you ever heard the devil's belittling voice in your head questioning who you are and why you're here? Well, this passage can help.

John the Baptist received the same line of questioning from the priests and Levites. And after stating that he was not the Christ, Elijah, or the Prophet, he answered them in a way that gives clarity to every Christ-follower concerning our identity and role in this world.

The prologue has concluded, and now we're moving into the narrative section the Gospel. And as we do, I want to ask you something.

Recently, I was traveling south along a road in my town. And I wanted to stay on it, but I found it hard to do. First, I had to slow down to go over a speed bump. Then, I had to make a hairpin turn to the right to get onto a different street because the one I'd been on suddenly became a one-way coming toward me. After making the hard right turn, I had to make an s-turn and stop. Then, I had to make a left onto another street and go through a roundabout before I was able to return to my original road and continue my journey.

That sounds an awful lot like religion to me.

That's what John was referring to when he used the term *wilderness* – the desolate condition of the Jewish faith at the time.

But, you know, it wasn't just about the Hebrews. In fact, it's always been – and perhaps always will be – that human beings drift toward religiosity. And religion always wants to make it hard for people to get to God. It wants the road to be as twisting, as torturous, as obstacle-ridden, as challenging as possible. And I guess that's because religionists want to feel like they have accomplished something difficult, and want to make sure that only the elite get in.

But that's not the heart of our God. That's not who we are. We are the ones who shout in this wilderness, "Make a straight path. Here he comes. He's on a rescue mission to save you."

This is who we are and why we're here – to say to a world that desperately needs Jesus Christ and his saving grace, "You don't have to jump through hoops and make hairpin turns and follow the roundabout. Just come to Jesus. Just bring your heart to him. He's waiting for you. There's a straight path."

Let's be the voices crying in the wilderness. Let's join John the Baptist in that understanding of who we are.

1:24-28 • The One Who is With Us

John answered them saying, "I baptize with water, but there stands One among you whom you do not know. It is He who, coming after me, is preferred before me, whose sandal strap I am not worthy to loose."
John 1:26-27

One day, a group of Pharisees approached John the Baptist and asked why he was baptizing people if he wasn't the Christ, Elijah, or the Prophet. And John answered them in a curious way. He told them about the one among them that they didn't know or, literally, didn't see. And then he went on to describe him as so great, so powerful, so awesome, so glorious that he wasn't worthy to even untie his shoes.

He was talking about Jesus who was likely in the crowd at the time. But they didn't know him, they didn't see him. And John was trying to say, "You're so focused on what I'm doing you're missing the point – the Son of God is with us!"

After reading this passage one afternoon, I stopped to reconsider how my day was unfolding, and I realized the same thing was happening to me. I'd become so engrossed in what I was doing I was becoming insensitive to the presence of Jesus.

So, I immediately stepped out onto the porch, took a seat in a wicker chair, and just listened to the rain for a while with an empty seat next to mine as a tangible reminder that right there, right then, in that very place, the one who promised to never leave me or forsake me was present. He always is. And that's what matters. The important thing is never what I'm doing, but the one who is with me when I'm doing it.

Maybe it would be a good idea for you to find a quiet spot today and just soak in his presence too.

1:29 • Sail Away

The next day John saw Jesus...and said, "Behold! The Lamb of God who takes away the sin of the world!
John 1:29

Wow! What a mouthful! Those two words, *takes away*, literally mean *to cause to sail away*. "Behold! The Lamb of God who *causes to sail away* the sin of the world!" I love that, because I need his forgiveness, and I'll bet you do too.

I used to live near the decommissioned Mare Island Naval Shipyards where for more than a hundred years, ships and submarines were built and launched. And the tower from an unfinished submarine still sits in front of one of the old drydocks as evidence of all the shipbuilding that went on there.

The U.S. Navy would build these massive vessels. And then once christened, they would slide down the slipway into the Napa River and sail away toward the horizon.

That's a lot like our sin. When we come to faith in Jesus, God's forgiveness causes it to slide into the great river of his grace and sail away into the horizon of his forgetfulness.

Did you know the Bible says that the God who knows everything that can be known has decided to forget your sin and mine (Hebrews 10:17)? He doesn't see you or me in the same frame as our sin. In fact, in another place, the Bible says he separates our sin from us as far as the east is from the west (Psalm 103:12). That's pretty far. That's the incredible forgiveness of our God.

Whatever guilt or shame you're dragging around with you today, bring it to the one whose forgiveness is greater than they are.

1:30-34 • Faith That's Real

And I have seen and testified that this is the Son of God.
John 1:34

In this passage, John the Baptist continued introducing his audience to Jesus as their long-awaited Messiah. He made it clear that although he always understood his ministry was about preparing the way for the Christ, as late as the previous day he had no idea who he was, where he would come from, or when he would arrive. But God had told him that he would recognize him by the sign of the Spirit descending and remaining on him.

And by the next day, John had witnessed this supernatural phenomenon. He described it as so substantial it was as though he had seen the Holy Spirit take on physical form. He said it was like a dove had landed and stayed on Jesus.

The three other Gospel writers – Matthew, Mark, and Luke – recorded that this happened at Jesus' baptism and that the voice of God was also audibly heard on that occasion declaring Jesus to be his beloved Son. So, it's no surprise then that John blurted out, "I have seen and testified that this is the Son of God."

His testimony was not based on wishful thinking, self-delusion, or metaphysics. It was faith for sure, but it was also empirical. His belief was tethered to his experience. And he had no alternative. He could do nothing else but proclaim the reality of what he'd seen and heard.

And I get that.

I became a Jesus-follower on the basis of my faith in what the Bible reveals about him. But my believing is also tightly linked with my experiencing. I too have seen and heard. My relationship with Christ is first and foremost a spiritual thing. But it's more than that. He has revealed himself to me in tangible, measurable, amazing ways. And I can't deny it. It's my story.

And our stories are powerful. That's why Revelation 12:11 says the devil is overcome by the blood of the Lamb – or the sacrifice of Jesus – *and* the word of our testimony. John the Baptist had a testimony, and that testimony – that story – is what God used to introduce his Son to a needy world.

God wants to do the very same thing with your story. He wants to reveal the Savior to those in the circle of your influence who need him and to use your testimony – the story of what you've seen and heard – to do it.

Don't discount the value of what you've experienced in Christ. You may not consider your testimony to be very dramatic. Maybe you haven't seen the Spirit descending like a dove or heard God's audible voice. But that's not the point. It's your genuineness that matters. People are hungry for faith that's real. And yours is. Jesus has changed your life. And simply sharing *that* with someone can have eternal impact.

Salvation is never based on someone's story, but it's often the result of hearing that story. I encourage you to share yours with someone today.

1:35-37 • The Voice and the word

The two disciples heard him speak, and they followed Jesus.
John 1:37

John the Baptist – who had previously described himself as the voice of one crying in the wilderness – was standing with two of his disciples. When he saw Jesus, he said to them, "Behold the Lamb of God!" And then it says his two disciples – John's two disciples – followed Jesus. And just like that, the Voice took a backseat to the word. And from then on, the ministry of John the Baptist faded to the background, and the ministry of Jesus took the foreground. And that's as it should be.

I travel frequently to a suburb of Taipei, Taiwan, called Danshui. And when I'm there, I'm reminded of the fact that it's really the word that's the important thing, not the voice. I don't speak Mandarin Chinese. And so, my attempts to communicate with locals are not very elegant. I kind of point and grunt and use exaggerated gestures hoping they will understand what I'm trying to say. But in the end, it's what I'm trying to say that's the important thing not, the way I say it. And that's true for us as believers.

But sometimes we lose sight of that.

We become enamored with the voice. We record it, video it, publish it, platform it with smoke and lights and guitars. We market, distribute, and promote it. And sometimes we forget that it's not the voice that matters. It's the word that matters.

May we remember what's important – Jesus, the word of God. As we seek to communicate him, let's take care not to promote the voice over the word.

1:38-39 • What Do You Seek?

Then Jesus turned, and ...said to them, "What do you seek?" They said to Him, "...Where are You staying?"
John 1:38

After two of John's disciples began to follow Jesus, he turned to them and asked, "What do you seek?"

This simple but searing question should cause all of us to stop and consider what we're looking for from the Lord?

If I'm honest, I have to say that a lot of what I seek from him is pretty selfish. I want comfort. I want encouragement. I want provision, and protection, and guidance. My prayers often sound more like the recitation of a shopping list, than a conversation with my loving Savior.

I don't think it's wrong to look to Jesus for those things. In fact, we shouldn't be looking to anything or anyone else for the meeting of those needs. But the satisfying of needs can't be the reason we follow Jesus.

These guys got it right. They were seeking to know where he was staying so they could be near him. They wanted to be where he was.

What do you seek from Jesus today? May we always simply seek to be where he is.

1:40-42a • Cross the Room

He first found his own brother Simon...and he brought him to Jesus.
John 1:41a & 42a

Andrew was one of two former disciples of John the Baptist that were now following Jesus. And we're told that one of the first things he did as a Christ-follower was to go find his brother, Simon Peter, and bring him to Jesus.

And I can't imagine anything more natural than for those of us who have encountered the saving grace of Jesus Christ to want to share it with those who don't yet know him, especially those we love. And yet, as I pondered that today, I had to honestly confess to myself and to God that at times, it's much easier for me to imagine sharing my faith with someone I don't know than it is to share with friends and family that are close to me.

A week ago, I performed a memorial service for a relative who'd passed away. As I prepared for it, I found myself becoming very anxious because I knew some of my relatives who don't yet know Jesus would be there. And I was nervous about how they would receive my gospel message. But the following day I got on a plane and flew to Taiwan where I would be sharing the gospel with strangers, and I wasn't anxious about it at all.

Along the riverfront in Danshui, Taiwan, there's a statue of a guy named, George Leslie Mackay. He was a medical doctor who in 1872 left his home in Canada, crossed the Pacific Ocean, landed at that point along the Danshui River in the northern part of Taiwan, and began sharing the gospel with people he'd never met – people who even spoke a different language than he did. It's a remarkable, bold, incredible story for which I'm very grateful. And the people of Taiwan are grateful enough that they erected the memorial to him.

But why is it so much easier for me to cross an ocean to share the good news with strangers than to cross the room and share with people I know well? I suppose it's because those who know me *know* me. They can immediately tell if my words match my life, and my testimony better ring true.

But they need the love of Jesus just as much as any stranger in another country. So, I've decided today to get my life in sync with my message, get over my fears, and boldly declare the amazing grace of God in Christ to everyone in the circle of my influence, including those who know me best.

1:42b • He Knows Your Name

You are Simon the son of Jonah. You shall be called Cephas...
John 1:42b

After Andrew introduced his brother, Simon, to Jesus, we're told that Jesus looked at him, called him by name, identified his father as the one who gave him that name, and then gave him a new name, Cephas, which means *stone* or *rock*.

This new identity stood in stark contrast to his given name of, Simon, which means, *hearing*, and gives the impression that perhaps he was someone who could listen all day to the opinions of others and never really arrive at one of his own — never really plant his feet solidly on anything.

But Jesus saw something in him that he didn't see in himself. The Lord was telling him, "Not only do I know the label you know yourself by, but I know where it comes from. I know who gave it to you. And your history does not dictate your future."

That's good for us to understand too!

I don't know about you, but I've had times when I've felt myself labeled by something I've done, or by the Accuser. And I've felt like maybe that's just who I am. But I'm grateful today to know that my Savior knows the real me. He sees me as who he made me to be, and never forgets that.

And that's true for you too. Perhaps you've come to believe your name is Failure, Insecure, Fearful, or any other of a multitude of names that may have been stamped on you by the devil or as the result of something you've done, or something you've been through.

If so, be reminded that there is a God in heaven who knows you — knows the real you — and is in the process of causing you to become everything he intended for you to become. He knows your name.

1:43-44 • Follow Him

The following day Jesus...found Philip and He said to him, "Follow Me."

John 1:43

Why is that so hard for us? Why is it so hard for *me*, to follow Jesus? It seems like most of the time I'd rather lead.

A lot of my praying is like this: "Lord, here's what I want to do, here's what I'd like to see happen, here are the goals I would like to achieve. Would you, please, make sure that it all works out just the way I envision without any hassles?"

I mean, seriously. How silly is that?

I think the reason why I have such a hard time following Jesus and try to assert myself into the lead position instead is because I forget that – like Philip – I was *found*. That means I was totally lost without him. Without Jesus, I didn't know where I was going. So, what gives me this notion that I can lead my own life?

Today, I want to tuck myself in behind my Savior. I want to live in his shadow and follow him – the one who knows where he's going, the one who knows what's best for my life. I want to *follow* him.

1:45-51 • Redirected

Before Philip called you, when you were under the fig tree, I saw you.
John 1:48b

Ionce had an office right next to some railroad tracks. And every day, massive freight trains came roaring down those tracks with such force that it literally shook the building. But not far from my door was a spot where that same huge locomotive could be redirected by something very simple called a switch. One man could move it and change the direction of the train. Something very simple can redirect a locomotive.

At the end of the first chapter of the Gospel of John, we have the record of a man's life being redirected by something very simple and yet massively profound. It's the story of Nathaniel. A guy named, Philip, who was his friend, found him and said, "Look, we've found the Messiah. It's Jesus of Nazareth." And Nathaniel's initial response was, "Can anything good come from Nazareth?"

He was expressing skepticism and even prejudice about the small, backwater, insignificant town that Jesus was from. And yet in a matter of moments, that same man would say to Jesus face to face, "You are the Son of God."

What changed his direction? What reoriented his life? Something that at first glance seems insignificant. Jesus told him, "Before you knew me, I knew you."

And there's not a more impactful – life-redirecting – truth in all the Bible than that. Those of us who are followers of Christ were chosen to become his adopted sons and daughters before the foundation of the world (Ephesians 1:4). Don't ask me to explain that, nobody can. But, the impact of it is simply awesome.

Think of it. The God and maker of all things, the master and sovereign of the universe saw me before I saw him and knew me before I knew him. Before I was anything, he thought I was something and set about to save me, set about to make it possible for me to be his child forever. That'll change your life. That'll redirect your path. That'll set you on a different course.

May it be that this simple reminder of the love of God who sought you before you were seeking him change your day and your life.

CHAPTER TWO

2:1-2 • The Ordinary Becomes Extraordinary

On the third day there was a wedding in Cana of Galilee...
John 2:1a

The second chapter of John opens with a wedding that Jesus attended along with his mother and his early group of disciples.

Weddings are kind of ordinary. But I don't mean they aren't special. We all love weddings. I have several on my calendar right now that I'm looking forward to being part of as either a guest or officiant. They're special in that way but ordinary in the fact that they take place all the time everywhere around the world. In fact, there's a venue a block from my home where outdoor weddings and receptions take place every single weekend during the spring and summer. They're ordinary in that sense.

But Jesus chose this ordinary event to unveil his extraordinary miracle power. He performed his first miracle at a wedding. He took something ordinary and made it extraordinary. And I have to ask myself the question, "Why a wedding in Cana, why there, why then?"

And of course, nobody can know for sure. But I wonder if it wasn't just the fact that he was invited there. And that makes me think, "How much of my ordinary life could become extraordinary if I simply invited Jesus to show up in those situations and circumstances?"

Today, my calendar is full of things I need to do and places I need to be. How often do I just go through my ordinary routine without a consideration that my ordinary life could become extraordinary if I simply invited Jesus into it?

What's on your calendar today? Are there soccer games for your kids? Are there appointments at work? Is there business travel? Is there time at the gym? What if you invited Jesus to show up there?

2:3-5 • Do What He Says

His mother said to the servants, "Whatever He says to you, do it."
John 2:5

These verses contain a conversation between Jesus and his mother about wine being served at a wedding, or more specifically, not being served at a wedding. It appears that Mary was related to the families involved and was serving as something of a wedding coordinator.

Jesus and his disciples had been invited to this wedding. But apparently, they showed up somewhere after the beginning of the week-long celebration. And by the time Jesus got there, Mary came to him to make sure he knew – speaking rather apologetically – that the wine had run out.

And then, she said something that sounds as though she thought Jesus could change the situation. He replied, "My time has not yet come," or "It's not my time yet."

That's a worthy study in and of itself. But what I'm focused on is what comes next when she made that incredible statement about doing what Jesus says.

I'm thinking about baptism, and you may be wondering why.

Water baptism is a lot of things – really important things. But among those – at the top of the list – it's a statement of obedience. You want to begin your life in Christ being water-baptized. And you want to begin that way because it sets the pattern for the life that's going to follow – one of obedience. At the root of it, we get baptized because Jesus said we should. And that's the way you want to live. You want to live your life every day doing whatever Jesus says.

Our problem is we often don't know what he's saying. Right? That's the thing. We think to ourselves, "If he would just make himself clear, I'm ready to obey."

I get that. I understand.

But on the other hand, I want to suggest something to you. Is there anything in the Bible that God has made clear you should do but you haven't yet? Perhaps it would be wise to start there. Just pick one of those commands and get your life aligned with it. Then, watch what he can do in response to your simple obedience.

2:6-10 • God's Budget

Jesus said to them, "Fill the waterpots with water." And they filled them up to the brim.
John 2:7

There was a television show being filmed down the street from my home. And the production company had erected a tent where the cast, crew, and extras were served their meals.

As I walked by one evening and noticed the delicious aromas, it reminded me of Jesus turning water into wine – his first miracle. It got me thinking about how the budget for the show probably provided for everything those folks needed. But that wasn't true for the wedding in Cana. They ran out of wine. They didn't have everything they needed. And Jesus' response to that was, "Give Me what you have."

What they had were six empty jars which could contain 20 to 30 gallons each. So, he instructed the servants to fill them with water – a colorless, tasteless, odorless liquid. Then, he told them to take a sample to the guy in charge of the feast. And when he tasted it, it was no longer water but wine – wine of the highest quality. So much so, the master of the feast responded, "You've saved the best for last."

Are you concerned about whether you'll have what you need for today? I don't know what that might be. I don't know what it is you're afraid you're lacking. But I know that God's budget is sufficient to cover everything. And I know that if you'll give him what you do have, whatever it may look like – however colorless, tasteless, odorless it might seem – he is able to take what you commit to him and make something fabulous out of it. Trust him.

2:9 • Delicious Secrets

When the master of the feast had tasted the water that was made wine, and did not know where it came from (but the servants who had drawn the water knew), the master of the feast called the bridegroom.
John 2:9

The master of the feast, who sampled the water that was now wine and pronounced it the best having been saved for last, did not know where it came from. Only the servants – the caterers – held that delicious secret.

Near my former home on Mare Island is a 150-year-old naval officer's mansion. And on the grounds is a small, separate cottage that was the servants' quarters. Thinking of that makes me wonder what it must have been like when the servants returned to their quarters that night and shared the amazing story with one another about water that became wine.

What a celebration they must have had! Remember, nobody knew that Jesus could perform miracles. He'd never done that before. There was zero expectation that when they poured all that water into the jars anything out of the ordinary would happen. And yet, they were on the front row of this amazing miracle that unfolded right before their eyes.

Last night, I was at the home of some people from church. We had some food and spent time celebrated the good things that Jesus is doing in our lives. And come on! Our God does some pretty amazing things – healing sick bodies, saving lost souls, providing material blessing for people in need. And when we have the chance to share those stories, it builds us up, strengthens us, and reminds us of what an amazing God we serve.

If you happen to be feeling a little down today, I encourage you to connect with some Christian friends and invite them to share their God stories. And don't neglect to return the favor so that all of you can enjoy the blessing of those delicious secrets.

2:11-12 • Glory on Display

This beginning of signs Jesus did in Cana of Galilee, and manifested His glory...
John 2:11a

The account of Jesus turning water into wine – his first miracle – closes by saying that through it, Jesus was putting His glory on display. It also says it was this manifestation of his glory that caused his disciples to believe in him – to cross the threshold from doubt into faith.

I think a lot of Christians imagine that presenting a well-crafted philosophical, theological, or intellectual argument for the existence and power of God would cause people to move from skepticism to faith. Or that somehow exposing them to the miraculous would do the trick. But most of the time, the thing that makes believers out of people isn't any of that. It's the glory of God.

Glory is a word that's hard to pin down with an airtight definition. But the best one I've ever heard is this: Glory is the divine word for beauty. And the beauty of God moves hearts to belief. I know that was true for me and probably for you too.

But how do you define the beauty of God? Well, it's his love. It's his mercy. It's his power. It's his wisdom. So many qualities are wrapped up in that phrase, *the beauty of God*. But there's also much more that's truly indescribable.

So, what is the Glory of God that moves people beyond their skepticism, doubt, and unbelief into faith? What is it that causes a heart to be inclined to follow after Christ as Savior? I don't think it can be adequately explained. So, how about joining me on the porch this evening as the sun sets in splendor. Instead of trying to use inadequate words to describe it, let me point to the horizon and let's gaze together at a reflection of it.

2:13-16 • A Beautiful Mess

When He had made a whip of cords, He drove them all out of the
temple, with the sheep and the oxen, and poured out the changers'
money and overturned the tables.
John 2:15

J esus went to Jerusalem to celebrate Passover. And when he
got there and entered the Temple, he found merchants selling
sacrificial animals as well as people engaged in currency
exchange. Both of these activities were allowed on the Temple
grounds by the religious leaders because they were seen to be
useful in assisting people with their worship. If you were a
pilgrim coming from a long distance, you wouldn't have to
bring your sacrifice with you. You could purchase one on site.
And if you were coming from a foreign country, you could
exchange your currency for the coin of the Temple and make a
financial contribution.

But, like most things we humans think we can institute to
enhance worship, they actually had become a stumbling block –
an impediment to worship. They'd become corrupt. And the
truth is, they just didn't belong there.

So, when Jesus showed up, it says he made a whip out of
cords and drove the sales people out of the Temple, set the
animals loose, and turned the tables of the money-changers
over sending coins rolling everywhere.

He made a royal mess – a beautiful mess.

And that reminds me of something that happened last
Sunday in one of our church's worship services. We were
singing songs of praise to the Lord and I felt the nudge of the
Holy Spirit to invite people to come to the front of the
auditorium. I didn't tell them why. But as soon as I made the
invitation, people started coming. As soon as they got there,

without any direction or instruction from me, they got on their knees. And this isn't our normal practice. So, it wasn't something they would have been expected to do.

And I knew immediately that the Holy Spirit was sweeping through making a beautiful mess clearing out junk that had become lodged in people's lives — sin that had accumulated, habits, activities, ideas, and ways of moving through life that had become impediments to worship.

I have to admit that I need that to happen periodically in my life too. I need the Lord to show up, set the animals loose, turn the tables over, and send the money rolling on the floor. And although it's not a pleasant process, the joy, peace, and freedom that results is absolutely wonderful.

Maybe today, you need the Lord to make a beautiful mess in your life. Just welcome him, won't you? Welcome him to do what he needs to, whatever it is.

2:17 • People Matter

Then His disciples remembered that it was written, "Zeal for Your house has eaten Me up."
John 2:17

When Jesus drove the merchants out of the Temple, it appears as though the disciples were somewhat stunned by the intense emotion and passion he displayed. It says that they processed all this by remembering something King David had written in Psalm 69. To paraphrase, it says, "Passion for your house – God's house – has consumed me."

They realized that this was what they were witnessing.

Here in the United States, we've just recently come through a bitterly divisive and contentious political season. People are still very angry and upset in every imaginable way, and it's pretty ugly.

I'm not saying the political issues aren't important. But isn't it interesting how people can get so worked up over things that aren't as important as God's house?

But what is God's house?

It's not a physical location. The Bible says that God doesn't dwell in temples made with human hands (Acts 17:24). It says that we – his people – are the temple of the Holy Spirit (1 Corinthians 6:19). So, I'd like to submit to you that what concerns God above all else – what really turns up the heat in his heart and consumes him – is you. You!

He's fiercely committed to you, to your well-being, to your wholeness, to his relationship with you. And anything that presents itself as an obstacle to that, he will come after with all the heat he can bring.

And that's something to take comfort in. But it's also something to pattern our lives after. Let's don't get our priorities mixed up. Let's stay focused on what matters to him. People matter to him.

2:18-23 • Signs

So the Jews answered and said to Him, "What sign do You show to us, since You do these things?"
John 2:18

There's a lot of talk about signs at the end of John chapter 2. The religious leaders wanted Jesus to perform a miraculous sign to prove that he had the authority to do what he had just done in cleansing the Temple. And Jesus, in effect, answered them by saying, "Well, how about this for a sign? After you crucify me, I'm going to rise from the dead on the third day."

They didn't really understand what he was talking about, so that didn't move the needle on their faith at all. But we're told the disciples heard him say it. And when he rose from the grave, they remembered it, and it strengthened their faith. In other words, the faith they had already placed in him was confirmed by the miraculous sign of his resurrection. That's important to remember.

This passage also describes a group of people there in Jerusalem during that Passover week who saw Jesus perform miraculous signs and believed in him as a result. But that means there were people there who saw him do those same miraculous signs and decided not to believe.

Signs are tricky things. I'm not saying that God doesn't want to perform them. The Bible is clear that he wants us to be able to experience his miraculous power. But when it comes to faith, it can't be on the basis of that.

Here's what I mean.

When we face things that are challenging or things that are drawing us to a decision point about whether we'll believe God, we want him to do or say something to make his will so obvious that we can trust him without exercising any actual...you know...faith.

But that's not how it works. Faith is a choice, always.

I know that we all long for demonstrations of his power. But it's been my experience that signs are nearly always given as confirmation of faith we've already placed in God rather than the reason for it.

What are the things that are calling for faith in your life today? What are the decision points of belief you're being drawn to? Are you facing something that will require you to choose whether you're going to trust God or not?

Understand that faith is a choice. Choose to believe him today.

2:24-25 • He Knows Me Best and Loves Me Most

But Jesus did not commit Himself to them, because He knew all men...
John 2:24

The chapter concludes by telling us Jesus did not commit himself to the crowds that were gathered in Jerusalem for Passover. He didn't entrust his security to them. And we're told why. He knows what's in us. He knows what's in man.

At first, that sounds a little sad, like he has a pretty low opinion of us. But that's not the case. In fact, we know that God sent Jesus to save us. The Heavenly Father thought you and I were valuable enough that we were worth the suffering and death of his son.

So, that's not what this is talking about. It's highlighting the fact that there's nothing I can hide from God. When God looks at my life, there aren't any hiding places. There are no shadows. He knows me fully. But that's a good thing.

I spend much of my life working to present a persona that I think will match the expectations of other people and put me in the best light and their good graces. And it's exhausting.

So, to know there's one person in this universe that I don't have to shape myself for, that I can tell my deepest, darkest secrets to and it won't change his opinion of me at all, and that I'm completely safe with is simply wonderful.

It reminds me of a line from an old song written by Bill and Gloria Gaither titled, *I Am Loved*: "The one who knows me best, loves me most."

CHAPTER THREE

3:1-3 • Seeing the Kingdom of God

...Unless one is born again, he cannot see the kingdom of God.
John 3:3b

The third chapter introduces Nicodemus. He was a religious leader and a ruler of the Jews. That meant he had power, authority, wealth, intelligence, and respect. He had everything anybody could want, but he was having his world rocked by Jesus. His teachings and miracles were affecting Nicodemus to the point where he decided to find out for himself who this guy was.

He sought him under the cloak of darkness so he wouldn't be seen by his fellow Pharisees. And when he reached Jesus, he said to him, "I know you're a teacher from God." But the Lord ignored his flattery and answered his unasked question instead. He said, "Unless a person is born again, they can't see the kingdom of God."

I imagine a man like Nicodemus would have thought he'd *seen* everything. But that wasn't true. Although Jesus would go on to explain more about what he meant, he was trying to help Nick understand he was oblivious to the kingdom of God. He told him the only way our eyes are open to that is by being born again.

And that reminds me of an occasion a couple of years ago when I was sitting next to a creek in one of the most beautiful places I'd been in a long time. The sound of the water was soothing. I was surrounded by monarch butterflies flitting here and there. The sun was out, and it was warm. And I could see glimpses of the Kingdom of God everywhere I looked.

I'm not talking about the natural beauty I was experiencing. Anyone would have been able to see and appreciate that. No, I'm referring to something infinitely more wonderful – the splendor of the realm of the King of Kings seeping into those precious moments by the stream. The glory of creation is merely a faint and marred reflection of the majesty of his domain. And in those moments, because I've been reborn into that kingdom, I was peering beyond what my eyes could resolve and treated to a sample of heaven.

There's a blindness we don't even know we have until we don't have it anymore. Being born again allows our eyes to be open to things we've never seen before – things beyond the veil sin has caused to limit our vision. And we find ourselves not only having been given access to the kingdom of God as our home in the ever after but the privilege of seeing its breakthroughs into the here and now.

Let's be sure to take in and enjoy the view today.

3:4 • It's All Downhill from There

Nicodemus said to Him, "How can a man be born when he is old?"
John 3:4a

J esus told Nicodemus that a person must be born again in order to see the Kingdom of God. And Nick replied by incredulously asking how a person could enter the womb a second time.

Have you ever found yourself telling God what's not possible? I do it all the time. "God, I can't afford that. I could never do that. They'll never agree to that." And on and on.

Why do we do it? It's so silly. We're talking about God. And once we've crossed the boundary from doubt into faith, we've left behind every restriction on what's possible. Once we believe in God, it's all downhill from there.

Look around. Everything you see is an impossibility. Life doesn't just spontaneously happen. Matter doesn't just appear from nothing. We believe in a God who created it all and is not limited by anything.

So, what sense does it make to insist that God be restricted by what we can understand or imagine? He's not limited in any way. And those things that he has invited you to trust him with or believe for are in the hands of the one for whom nothing is impossible (Luke 1:37).

3:5-7 • Paradigm Reshaped

That which is born of the flesh is flesh, and that which is born of the Spirit is spirit.
John 3:6

In chapter 3 verse 5, Jesus repeats himself. He doesn't do that very often. And he shouldn't have to. He's the Son of God. So, if he says something once, that ought to be the end of the story. But here, having already told Nicodemus that, "Unless a person is born again, they can't see the Kingdom of God," he says nearly the same thing again.

Both times, he begins by saying, "Most assuredly," or, "Most emphatically, I say this to you." So, this is serious. It's important.

He's trying to help Nicodemus understand what it means to be born again because even though Nicodemus is a religious leader, this is shattering his religious paradigm. And even people like you and me who have been born again need to have our paradigm reshaped from time to time because we can find ourselves drifting to one of two concepts about being born again that aren't true.

One of them is that it's like a "do-over" – that we just get a second chance at trying to get it right. That's not being born again. Neither is it like adding cheese and bacon to your basic burger and making it a deluxe. We don't just add Jesus to our lives and get something somewhat better.

In fact, in verse 6, Jesus said, "That which is born of the flesh is flesh." It's never going to be anything else but flesh. The life I used to live – the life controlled, dominated, and led by my flesh – cannot see the Kingdom of God. It must be left completely behind. "That which is born of the Spirit is spirit."

When we cross the threshold from doubt into faith, we don't

drag our flesh-life with us. We are truly born again. That's why 2 Corinthians 5:17 says that we who have come to faith in Christ are a new creation.

That's good news! We can't work our way into the Kingdom of God – the realm where God rules. So, let's stop trying. Our flesh can never ever get us there. But the new birth – by faith in Christ – does.

3:8 • Raising a Sail

The wind blows where it wishes...So is everyone who is born of the Spirit.
John 3:8

J esus said being born of the Spirit is like the wind. It goes where it wants to. You hear the sound of it, but you don't know where it came from, and you don't know where it's going. And that reminds me of sailboats.

I love vacationing in the Hawaiian Islands. I get there on an airplane that expends an incredible amount of energy to break the bonds of gravity and push its way across the Pacific Ocean to deposit me on the beach. But the people who originally came to those islands didn't get there that way. They simply raised a sail and let the wind bear them along.

And our life in Jesus – being born of the Spirit – is supposed to be a lot more like that. That's what Jesus said. And yet many of us have adopted an airplane model of Christianity. We use a lot of energy to push ourselves along the path that we think the Holy Spirit wants us to go. And it's wearying. How much better to just raise the sail and let him carry us to where he's going?

Today, I invite you to Join me in raising a sail.

3:9-12 • Steps of Faith

*If I have told you earthly things and you do not believe, how will you
believe if I tell you heavenly things?*
John 3:12

J esus had been trying to explain to Nicodemus what it means
to be born again. But you get the impression Nick was kind
of stuck – that he was having trouble taking that initial step of
faith. There was more Jesus wanted to lead him into – more
that he wanted for him to experience. But until he took the step
in front of him, he couldn't get to the one after that.

And that makes me wonder about those times in my life
when I feel like my faith journey has stalled out a bit. I wonder
if maybe the reason is that I'm trying to skip a step – trying to
get to the next one without taking the one directly in front of
me. The Bible says that our spiritual development is "line upon
line" (Isaiah 28:10). We can't skip any of the steps. They're all
important.

I remember when Jesus was trying to teach me about tithing
– the practice of giving ten percent of my income to him. Yikes!
That was so beyond what I could grasp in faith. But he was
showing me through his word that it would release me from the
grip of materialism and unleash his blessing on my life. Still, I
struggled with it. And the result was my spiritual development
slowed to a crawl. But once I took that step, I discovered there
was one after that I could take, and one after that, and one after
that.

So, if you feel sort of stuck today, perhaps there's a step of
faith you need to take. I don't know what it might be, but I
encourage you to take it. Take that step, and then the one after
that, and then the one after that, and the one after that.

3:13 • He is with Us

*No one has ascended to heaven but He who came down from heaven,
that is, the Son of Man who is in heaven.*
John 3:13

This is a continuation of Jesus' conversation with Nicodemus. He referred to himself as the Son of Man and established his bona fides as the one and only savior. But his choice of language also introduced Nicodemus to the truth of God's omnipresence. That means that God is everywhere at once.

Jesus was explaining to him that at the same time he was standing there, he was also in Heaven. There was no difference to him. He was with Nicodemus and in his eternal realm of glory seated on his sovereign throne all at the same time.

This is such a difficult concept for us to grasp because we are so rivetted to time and space. If I'm in Hawaii, I'm not at home in California. If I want to be in California, I have to leave Hawaii. I'm not in more than one place at a time.

But Jesus is.

He doesn't have to travel anywhere. When I pray to him, my prayers don't have to make their way through some process to find him. When I cry out to him for his presence, his help, or his aid, he doesn't have to traverse any territory – any geography – to get to me. He is with me.

He's with us right now. And not in some token way. No, he is with us in all of his eternal glory, power, wisdom, and love. He is with us.

3:14-15 • Sin for Us

And as Moses lifted up the serpent in the wilderness, even so must the Son of Man be lifted up...
John 3:14

We have reached the basecamp from which we will summit the towering peaks of chapter 3 verses 16 and 17. But here, Jesus reminds Nicodemus of something that he would have been very familiar with as a Hebrew scholar and Jewish leader – the story of when Moses in the wilderness raised a pole with an emblem of a poisonous serpent on it (Numbers 21:4-9).

You see, the Children of Israel, because of fear, had refused to enter the Promised Land – the place that God had promised them as their inheritance. As a result, they began what would become forty years of wandering in the wilderness. But instead of acknowledging their own faithlessness, they started to blame God for the challenging circumstances that resulted. And this unleashed a judgment upon them. Poisonous serpents were causing people to die.

But God was unwilling to leave them in that predicament even though they brought it on themselves. He instructed Moses to make a bronze serpent – an image of the very thing that was killing them – and raise it up on a pole. He said that anyone who would look at it would be rescued. They would be healed. They would be recovered. And they were.

So, when Jesus told Nicodemus he was going to have to be lifted up in a similar way, he was describing his coming death on the cross. He was saying that he was going to become the one sinners could look to for rescue. He would create the opportunity for people to not perish but have everlasting life.

He was referring to the fact that he would be made sin for

us. That's what 2 Corinthians 5:21 says. He was made to look like my sin and yours. He took upon himself the full weight of the wicked condition of humankind and bore it to the cross so that we could be rescued, recovered, redeemed and live with him for eternity.

I am in awe today of a God who loves me so much that he was willing to take on my sin – to become sin for me – so that I no longer have to bear it.

3:16-17 • The Football Verse

For God so loved the world that He gave His only begotten Son, that whoever believes in Him should not perish but have everlasting life. For God did not send His Son into the world to condemn the world, but that the world through Him might be saved.
John 3:16-17

These verses are so clear, so profound, so majestic, so full of grace that they certainly don't need my commentary. So, having quoted them, I'll just allow them to stand over us as the towering peaks of God's word that they are.

But I can't help getting just a little emotional right now because these are the first words I remember hearing from the Bible as a young child. So, they've been with me for a long time. They introduced me to the God who loves me. And they escorted me across the threshold of faith into the forgiveness of my Redeemer. So, I can't stop myself from being deeply moved as I consider them all over again.

And I hope that never changes.

The other day, I heard a friend refer to John 3:16 as the *football verse*. And I knew exactly what she meant. We've all seen someone holding up a hand-lettered sign from the stands at a televised football game hoping to catch the camera's eye and stir a viewer's curiosity to consider Christ.

I honor those who do that. And I know my friend's comment was not meant disrespectfully toward either the sign-maker or the verse. But her statement got me thinking and served as a much-needed reminder for me to not become so familiar with God's amazing grace that I ever treat it casually.

May the power of God's love always cause my throat to tighten with emotion, my eyes to leak, and my knees to bend in humble worship before so great a God.

3:18-21 • Doing the Truth

But he who does the truth comes to the light...
John 3:21a

Jesus concludes his conversation with Nicodemus by saying that those who choose not to put their faith in him as Savior do so because they don't want their evil deeds exposed by his light. And after having already made it clear that he had not come to condemn people, he said that those who choose not to step into the light are condemning themselves...to remain in the dark.

I spent the first 35 years of my life as a perfectionist, a control-freak, and a workaholic. Instead of dragging those behaviors out into Christ's light where they would be exposed for the evil and sin that they were, I chose to congratulate myself for how much I could accomplish, my work ethic, and my standards of excellence. But that only served to keep me trapped in those behaviors and nearly caused the loss of my marriage and ministry as well as my health.

During that dark time, I came across a book titled, "We Are Driven: The Addiction America Applauds." I know the Lord arranged for me to encounter that book. And as I stared into the truth it contained, I began to reconsider the shadows where I'd been living.

It wasn't until I was willing to step out of the darkness of denial and become one who *does the truth* – as verse 21 says – that I began to experience the cleansing and recovery that only Christ's forgiveness accomplishes. My life began to change. My *deeds* began to shine with the very light of God that I had once resisted.

In this passage, Jesus makes it clear that it has always been this way, but surely no more so than now. People work very hard to keep their sin covered. We want our evil legalized, validated, excused, even celebrated. But as we do, we're only sentencing ourselves to remain in that darkness.

Let's break that cycle and become determined to respond to the conviction of the Holy Spirit by immediately bringing our iniquity out into the light of confession and faith in our loving Savior so that we can be transformed.

3:22-26 • Jealousy, Comparison, and Competitiveness

And they came to John and said to him, "Rabbi, He who was with you beyond the Jordan, to whom you have testified — behold, He is baptizing, and all are coming to Him!"
John 3:26

This section of chapter 3 is the setup for a lengthy and very powerful response from John the Baptist to his disciples who are concerned that Jesus is beginning to take the spotlight away from him. You see, Jesus, who had just recently been baptized by John and begun his public ministry, had moved downriver a relatively short distance, and his disciples had begun to baptize people too.

So, you have this awkward period where both John and Jesus are preaching a message that people are responding to with repentance evidenced by being baptized in water. And John's disciples were thinking, "Well, maybe our guy is becoming irrelevant. And if so, what does that say about us, our place in the world, our value."

I'll deal with John's speech in more detail later. But these initial verses introduce the subject of jealousy, comparison, and competitiveness. And those three sisters are extremely corrosive to our souls. But all of us know what it's like to have one or more of them come calling. In fact, I'd like to tell you about a serious run-in I had with them.

Here's some context.

For several years I'd been working to establish and then lead a vibrant, healthy, men's ministry in our church. As we began seeing real traction in this area, I was able to hand the leadership of it over to one of the guys who'd been helping me. And he did a great job. So much so, that I could just show up for the meetings without having any responsibilities at all. And it was wonderful on one hand but very challenging on the other.

It was wonderful to see the fruit of my labors. But I found myself having to deal with the temptation to entertain jealousy, comparison, and competitiveness because the ministry was actually doing better without me. There were more guys attending, engagement was higher, worship was stronger. And I found myself thinking, "OK, why is the new leader better than me?" And then, that turned into, "What's wrong with me?" I began to question my worth and wonder if I'd become irrelevant.

Has anything like that ever happened to you? Have you had someone step into the frame of your life who seemed better looking, more capable, smarter, or more effective than you and found yourself dealing with jealousy, comparison, and competitiveness?

The devil wants to try and snare us with that temptation because there's no good that comes from it. There's no path to a true sense of self-worth that follows that road. It only leads to discouragement and self-defeating attempts to become someone other than the person God uniquely made us to be.

There's only one way you and I are meant to develop a healthy self-image and secure a sense of self-worth. It has to be based on how God values us. And he's made it clear that he considers us so valuable we were worth the sufferings of the cross. Wow! Just consider that for a minute.

And that's what I experienced one morning at one of our men's gatherings. In the midst of the rising temptation to think otherwise, I heard the familiar voice of the Holy Spirit reminding me that I'm treasured by the only one whose assessment truly matters. And I found myself confessing the pride and insecurity that I'd been giving place to.

Then, my heart heard – all over again – my Heavenly Father say to me, "I love you, son." And in an instant, jealousy, comparison, and competitiveness evaporated from my soul.

So, if you've found yourself surrendering to the seduction of this demonic triad, don't take one more step down that path. Confess this as the sin it is and repent of it right now. Remember the message of the cross: You are loved!

3:27 • The Evil and the Ugly

A man can receive nothing unless it has been given to him from heaven.
John 3:27

This is the Baptist's response to his followers who were concerned that Jesus was upstaging him. And he essentially said, "Look, I don't have any claim to fame here. There isn't anything of prominence or ministry that I'm perceived to have that isn't a gift from God."

I love John for his heart and humility.

It makes me think about the things I consider to be my own that really aren't. I'll talk about my life, my future, my health, my family, my talents, and so on. But none of those things are really mine. Every good thing that has become part of me is a gift from God. And I never want to forget that.

To be honest, the only things I can really claim as my own are the evil and the ugly. It's correct for me to refer to my sin, my selfishness, my lust, and my prejudice. That's a nasty list, but those are the kind of things I can claim.

I've been forgiven, and I'm so grateful to God that he doesn't see that stuff in me anymore. He sees the forgiveness of Christ over me. But I never want to forget where the good things in my life come from.

3:28 • The Setup Man

You yourselves bear me witness, that I said, "I am not the Christ,"
but, I have been sent before Him.
John 3:28

J ohn the Baptist continued his response to his followers by
essentially saying, "You guys could stand before a judge in a
court of law and give testimony to the fact that in everything I
say and do, Jesus is first. He is honored. You know that I live
what I believe. I'm just the setup man. I'm just the guy who
goes before and prepares the way."

John's words here cause a question to form in my mind that
I just can't shake. I need to answer it. And that question is this:
Does my life and the way I live it distract from or focus
attention on Jesus?

Could I go to the people who know me best, look them in
the eye, and with a straight face say, "You know that I'm careful
with my words so they always honor Jesus, and his impact on
my life is so great, that even the things I do reflect my passion
for him"?

I'm not sure I could do that yet. But thank God, my story is
not finished. The Holy Spirit is still at work in my life. And I'm
determined to submit to his shaping influence so that my words
and deeds will increasingly reflect Jesus. I want others to desire
to follow him because of what they see of him in me.

Your story isn't finished yet either. And if you share my
desire, let's prayerfully walk in the footsteps of the Baptist today
allowing the Spirit to make the testimonies of our lives more
like his.

3:29 • The Best Man

Therefore this joy of mine is fulfilled.
John 3:29b

Alright, I admit it. When it comes to amusement parks, especially Disneyland, I'm just a big kid at heart. I get a lot of joy and pleasure out of not only the attractions but the atmosphere itself. But I'll be the first to say that those joyful experiences only last about as long as the ride I'm on like Pirates of the Caribbean or Space Mountain. It's certainly not a fulfilling joy, not a complete joy in any way. It's still great, but it's not that.

So, when I read that John the Baptist said his joy is fulfilled – his joy bucket is a full as it can be – that makes me take notice. I want to know what produces that kind of complete joy in a person's life? And he said it's this: To be the best man at the wedding – to stand next to the groom.

He was clearly talking about Jesus and that his bride is those he loves – his Church, you and me, those he saved and redeemed.

John said to stand next to the groom – to be close enough to hear the sound of his voice as he gushes over his bride – is what causes the joy that fills. This is the joy that completes.

I want that. I don't want my life to be a pursuit of temporal joy but the kind that completely satisfies. I want to be near enough to my Savior – near enough to the action of his saving grace and the drawing of his bride to himself – that I experience what John described.

3:30 • I Must Decrease

He must increase, but I must decrease.
John 3:30

This is such a succinct and profound statement of truth. John the Baptist was continuing to try to describe for his followers what was happening. A transition was going on where the prominence of the ministry of Jesus was increasing and his own diminishing.

I think that sometimes when people read these words or hear them read, they imagine that John was engaging in some kind of grand and noble act of humility where he was stepping into the wings and giving Jesus the stage. But that's not the case at all. In fact, he made that clear when he said, "He *must* increase."

This is the Son of God he was talking about. He owns the room. It's his stage. It's his show. John was clarifying that he was merely a spectator in an amazing display of the glory and grace of God.

And when he talked about himself needing to decrease, he wasn't talking about his value to God. He wasn't talking about his worth. He was talking about his role, that the right way to live – the only course of life that makes sense – is to tuck oneself in behind the one whose name is on the marquee. That's where life is lived best, when we recognize Jesus is Lord.

3:31 • Eternal Perspective

He who comes from above is above all; he who is of the earth is earthly and speaks of the earth.
John 3:31a

John the Baptist referred to himself as one who only sees things from a ground-level perspective. But he made it clear that Jesus is from Heaven. He is above all. His view is unobstructed.

In Isaiah chapter 55 verse 9, God says of himself, "As high as the heavens are above the earth, so are my ways and my thoughts above yours."

And that's good to know, because every single day of my life I'm confronted by choices I need to make and situations I need to deal with that require a broader view than my own. I'm from the earth as well. My perspective is obstructed in every direction. I can only see so far.

It's like a mouse in a maze. It's guesswork at best. I don't know which way to go. But, the one who loves me most and always has my best interests in mind is also the one who knows the end from the beginning – whose perspective is eternal in every direction. He knows exactly what to do in every situation and can be trusted with the affairs of my life.

So, right now I choose to do exactly that, look to him for the guidance and direction that I need, and to trust him for the wisdom that's required in every situation I face.

Care to join me?

3:32-36 • A Full Dose

For God does not give the Spirit by measure.
John 3:34b

The last five verses of this chapter are the conclusion of John the Baptist's powerful speech we've been considering. And for the most part, these verses deal with themes we've already discussed except for the last part of verse 34.

I think a lot of people imagine the Holy Spirit to be like a substance that can be dispensed in differing quantities or in varying concentrations as though you could get more or less of him or be given a more or less potent dose of him.

But he's a person not a thing, and he's either with us or he's not.

And the Lord made clear how important the in-dwelling presence of the Spirit is. He told his disciples it was to their advantage that he return to the Father so he could send the Holy Spirit to them (John 16:7), and that the Holy Spirit would supply the power they would need to become his witnesses (Acts 1:8).

Then, on the Day of Pentecost, when the Spirit was poured out on the first believers, Peter stood up and said this experience was not just for a select group but for every believer (Acts 2:39).

Near my home, some old buildings are being remodeled and restored to house a distillery and its tasting room. I don't drink alcohol, so I don't have firsthand knowledge of this, but I imagine that when people come to visit there, they will only be given a small sample of the distilled spirits to taste.

Pardon my crude analogy, but you have not been given a sample of the Holy Spirit. You have been given the entire cask.

You have received his fullness.

If you're a follower of Jesus, he inhabits you fully. That means there is nothing – no challenge you could ever face – that would overwhelm his power in you. There's nothing you could ever walk through – no experience you could ever have – that would be greater than the force of his comfort to console and carry you.

You have not been given the Spirit by measure. Drink your fill.

CHAPTER FOUR

4:1-4 • It's Always About the Journey

But He needed to go through Samaria.
John 4:4

Jesus determined to leave Judea in the southern part of Israel and return to his home region of Galilee up in the North. But the statement in verse 4 that he *needed* to go through Samaria is curious.

Palestine was divided into three sections: Judea in the South where Jerusalem was, Galilee in the North where the Sea of Galilee and Nazareth were, and then between the two was the region of Samaria. But the Samaritans were not Jews. In fact, the Jews hated them. So much so, that when traveling between Judea and Galilee, many would go completely around Samaria to avoid having any interaction with them. So even though Samaria would have been the most direct route for Jesus to take, it wouldn't have been the only choice, and perhaps not even the one most expected.

So why does it say, "He *needed* to go through Samaria"? Well, we're going to find out because in the next few verses we're going to hear about an amazing encounter Jesus had with a woman at a well outside the city of Sychar in Samaria. Her life was dramatically impacted along with everybody in her whole town as well as the disciples.

This causes me to think about my own life and my own faith journey. I'm often so focused on what I'm leaving behind and where I hope to be headed that I forget about the path between the two. And I become unavailable for the experiences I *need* to have, the lessons I *need* to learn, and the people I *need* to encounter, along the way. But with Jesus, it's always about the journey, because it's those things that we pass through along the way that make the destination not only possible but meaningful.

So, I invite you to join me in choosing to be less concerned with our departure and destination points. Let's decide instead to follow our Savior along the path of his choosing and drain every drop out of every moment along the way.

4:5-6 • Take a Break

Jesus, therefore, being wearied from the journey, sat thus by the well.
John 4:6b

As Jesus traveled from Judea to Galilee, he became
sufficiently tired from the journey that upon reaching the
city of Sychar in Samaria, he sat down to get a drink of water
and just take a break.

Do you know what it's like to be weary, to be physically
exhausted, mentally fatigued, or emotionally drained? I certainly
do. And Jesus does too. He knows exactly what it's like to live
within the limitations of flesh and blood. He has first-hand
experience with being human because even though he was
never less than fully God, he was also fully man.

The Bible says that God never forgets we're dust (Psalm
103:14). And that's not a put-down. That's a loving God saying,
"I never expect you to be anything more than what I made you.
I don't expect you to be super-human."

I don't know about you, but I put that expectation on myself
a lot. I want to be a super-husband, a super-pastor, a super-dad.
But I'm not. I'm just me. There are times when I simply reach
the limit of my capacities. And it's comforting to know at those
times that I can crawl up into my Savior's lap, put my head on
his strong chest, and just recover knowing he welcomes that.

Perhaps you need some recovery today. I do. Let's come to
the well of his living water, put our feet up for a while, and let
him restore us.

4:7-9 • The Power of Being Regarded

Then the woman of Samaria said to Him, "How is it that You, being a Jew, ask a drink from me, a Samaritan woman?"
John 4:9a

When Jesus reached Jacob's Well outside Sychar, he had a wonderful conversation with a Samaritan woman. And it began very simply. He just asked her for a drink of water. But she was so astonished – so amazed that he even spoke to her – she asked him, "Why are you talking to me?"

And there were at least a couple of reasons why she may have been surprised by that. First, he was a Jew, she was a Samaritan, and the two groups didn't get along. So, she wouldn't have expected that he would address her civilly at all. And then there's the likelihood borne out by the context of the rest of the chapter that she was a woman who was ostracized by her peer group – the other women in town – because of her reputation for sleeping around. That's why she was there drawing water alone instead of coming with the rest of the ladies.

So, she would have been used to not being spoken to. She would have been used to being disregarded.

But Jesus reached across that chasm and simply talked to her. And that act alone set in motion the falling of the dominoes so that by the end of their conversation, she, and then ultimately her whole town, came to faith in Jesus as Messiah.

And that makes me think about something that happened just the other day. I was out for a walk in the park and I came across a guy sitting on the curb. I assumed he was homeless. He had a ragged suitcase at his feet, and he was just barking at the moon – just shouting out nonsensical things. So, I presumed he was either high on something or mentally disturbed in some way. I just walked on by, didn't acknowledge him in anyway, and just gave him a wide berth.

I'm not sure I would have or should have done anything else, but it makes me wonder why it's so easy for me to just disregard people – to act like they're not even there. As I move through the course of my day, there are lots of people that cross my path that I don't even acknowledge. How can that be?

I wonder how many people who populate the fringes of the circle of my life's influence would be astonished if I simply spoke to them. And how many of them might come to faith in Jesus and know his amazing grace if I did?

Lord Jesus, help me represent you better in this world.

4:10 • What are You Thirsty for?

If you knew the gift of God, and Who it is Who says to you, "Give me a drink," you would have asked Him, and He would have given you living water.
John 4:10b

J esus continued his conversation with the woman who came to draw water at the well by saying in a sense, "Ma'am, you don't even know who you're talking to. If you did, you'd bring him that thirst you can't even name and find in him the satisfaction you seek by means you can't even imagine."

Some time ago, I was emptying the waste basket under my desk. As I took it outside to the main garbage can, I noticed something. It was full of empty, plastic, Starbucks Frappuccino cups. And I was struck. I was in one of those moments where God was arresting my attention. And I found myself asking, "Randy, what are you thirsty for? Whatever it is, these coffee drinks aren't cutting it."

I won't tell you the rest of that story now. It ends well. But let me ask you. What are you thirsty for? Do you even know? What is your soul longing for that you can't even name?

If I looked in the garbage can under your desk would I find the remains of attempts to satisfy that thirst? If I looked in your internet browsing history would I find trails to porn and gambling sites – places you've visited trying to satisfy that longing that you don't even understand? What if I looked in your closet? Would I see clothes in there that you bought thinking they would do it – they would make you feel special – but they didn't so they just hang in your closet unworn? If I looked in your garage, would I find a car payment sitting there that's become a financial noose around your neck and never fulfilled its promise to make you happy?

We often look in the wrong places to find what will satisfy our souls because we don't even know what we need. So, let me ask again. What are you thirsty for? Even though you may not have an answer to that question, there is someone who does. His name is Jesus. And he's the only one with the living water that can quench it. Bring your thirst to him today.

4:11-14 • Grace Like a Firehose

*...Whoever drinks of the water that I shall give him will never thirst.
But the water that I shall give him will become in him a fountain...*
John 4:14:a

As the Samaritan woman was processing what Jesus said about living water, he went on to tell her that it not only quenches spiritual thirst but becomes a fountain. And that reminds me of John 7:37b-38 where Jesus said, "If anyone thirsts, let him come to Me and drink...out of his heart will flow rivers of living water."

You see, the amazing grace of Jesus Christ that flows to my thirsty soul, satisfies every longing, and brings my spirit to life is not meant to end with me. It's not meant to stop there. It's meant to flow through me to the parched souls of all those who surround my life.

And that reminds me of a trip that my wife and I took years ago to the Dead Sea in Israel. It's called the Dead Sea because water flows into it from the Jordan River, but it has no outlet. So, the water stagnates. Over the millennia, it has become so salty it won't support life.

And that's a powerful picture of what happens to people like you and me when we try to horde the grace of God. It's not meant to be just about our own salvation. God wants us to become like pipelines, fountains, rivers of living water through which his amazing grace flows to others.

So, I invite you to join me today in asking the Lord to give us sensitivity to those who are thirsty. And let's allow his living water to flow through us to them. May they experience his grace like a firehose.

4:15-18 • Have that Conversation

You have well said, "I have no husband," for you have had five husbands, and the one whom you now have is not your husband; in that you spoke truly.
John 4:17b-18

Jesus' conversation with the woman at the well took a very surprising turn. He'd been talking to her about how the living water that he can offer will satisfy the longing of the human soul. And although she was still processing that a bit, she asked him to give her some.

And then, out of the blue, he said to her in response, "Go call your husband."

What? What did he just say? Why did he say that? What does that have to do with anything?

She told him she wasn't married. And his response was, "That's right. In fact, you've been married five times, and the guy you're living with right now is not your husband."

Oh boy! I don't think she wanted to have that conversation with Jesus. But she desperately needed to. She was caught, like so many of us, in a repetitive cycle of behavior that was at least unsatisfying and probably destructive. She likely just kept telling herself that although she'd made a mistake with the last guy, the next one would be *Mr. Right.* But of course, it never works out that way.

I refer to it as the *broken-record syndrome.* Back in the ancient days of vinyl records, if the platter would get scratched in some way, the needle traveling the grooves and reproducing the sound would hit that scratch and skip. And that often meant it would just repeat the same passage of music over, and over, and over, and over again.

A lot of us know what that's like. We find ourselves unable

to escape these patterns in our lives – our attempts to deal with stuff we don't even understand and can't seem to break free from.

I know it's hard. We don't like to visit those painful places. But unless we're willing to let Jesus expose the roots of our bondage – unless we're willing to go there with him and let him speak truth to us about what's really going on in our lives – then his living water can't penetrate to that parched area in our souls. It can't get there.

But on the other side of that very challenging conversation with Jesus that deals with the real issues of our lives, there is so much freedom – so much wholeness.

If you sense Jesus raising a topic you don't want to discuss, I encourage you. Have that conversation. Let him take you there.

4:19-26 • The One who Can Heal What's True

God is Spirit, and those who worship Him must worship in spirit and truth.
John 4:24

The woman at the well told Jesus he must be some kind of prophet. A prophet speaks or reveals truth. But Jesus clarified that he's more than a prophet, he's the Messiah – the one who can heal what's true.

She then tried to distract attention away from the truth he'd just revealed concerning the brokenness of her soul. And she did this by attempting to draw him into a debate about a religious controversy. She said, "We Samaritans believe we're supposed to worship on this mountain. You Jews say we're supposed to worship in Jerusalem."

But Jesus didn't take the bait. He told her none of that matters. It's not important *where* we worship. What matters is *how* we worship. God is looking for those who will worship him in *spirit* and *truth* – both together – not one without the other. Real worship happens when our spirits reach out to God with a sincere acknowledgement about the truth of our need for him.

I've noticed something. And perhaps you have too. Some of the people who appear the most spiritual by engaging in religious talk, activity, and arguments are really just working hard to hide or not deal with their own brokenness. They're living in denial and trying to draw attention away from it.

Their worship my even seem to be in *spirit*. But without *truth*, it's incomplete. And it doesn't help anything.

It's not until we're willing to acknowledge the truth of the reality of our need that we find Jesus is more than a prophet. He's the Messiah – the one who can heal what's true.

4:27-30 • The Forgotten Water Pot

The woman then left her waterpot...
John 4:28a

The woman Jesus had been ministering to returned to the city of Sychar specifically to tell the people there that she had met the Messiah. And we're given this very interesting factoid. We're told that when she left Jesus, she also left her waterpot. It just sat there as silent testimony to the fact that after meeting Jesus, the thing she got up that morning thinking was the driving priority of her day didn't really matter so much.

And boy, have I found that to be true! Living in relationship with my Savior has caused things that once absorbed my attention and demanded my time to be almost immaterial. They don't matter. Jesus matters. His priorities matter. His presence matters. The rest, not so much.

And that reminds me of a song I learned as a kid growing up in church, a hymn really. It was written by a woman named, Helen Lemmel. In 1922, she wrote these lyrics:

Turn your eyes upon Jesus
Look full in his wonderful face
And the things of earth will grow strangely dim
In the light of his glory and grace

What are the things that are driving you today? What are the things that are frightening you today? What are the things that are screaming for your attention today? I invite you to turn from them, take a long, steady look into the eyes of Jesus, and experience what happens when you do.

4:31-34 • The Food that Feeds

But He said to them, "I have food to eat of which you do not know...My food is to do the will of Him who sent Me, and to finish His work."
John 4:32 & 34b

In chapter 4 verses 31 to 34 there is a very interesting juxtaposition. The Samaritan woman returned *to* the city of Sychar having had her spiritual thirst quenched right after the disciples had returned *from* the same city to offer Jesus food to satisfy his physical hunger.

But when the disciples pressed him to eat something, he taught them about a different kind of food.

He wasn't saying his physical body didn't need nutrition. He was trying to teach his disciples about the true source of the fulfillment, purpose, meaning, and transcendence we all hunger for. And there's nothing we can feed ourselves that will supply these.

Early in Jesus' ministry, we're told that he was tempted three times by the devil. And the first of those temptations was to turn stones into bread after he had been fasting for forty days. He resisted that temptation by quoting from the Old Testament (Deuteronomy 8:3) saying, "Man shall not live by bread alone..." (Matthew 4:4b)

The life we were created for is nourished by something more than food could ever provide.

We were meant to be partners with God – to participate with him in what he's doing. In fact, in the book of Genesis, one of the first things we see about Adam in the Garden of Eden is God involving him in what he was doing – inviting him to share in his creative processes – by assigning him to catalog the animal kingdom.

We were meant for more.

And that's why today people are starving for meaning, hungry for purpose. And that's also why one of the hottest trends in marketing is to tie the sale of goods and services to a cause by contributing a percentage of the sale to a charitable organization. And that's certainly commendable.

But ultimately, there's only one cause that matters: the cause of Christ. Why? Because until people's lives are transformed by his gospel, every form of philanthropy will fall short. However, when people's hearts are changed, everything else changes. We treat each other differently. We treat the environment differently. Our priorities are different.

And being involved in making that happen is what brings true fulfillment, meaning, purpose, and transcendence.

So if you, like me, long for more than the meager fare this world is serving up, let's become engaged in the work of him who sent us. Let's preach the gospel.

4:35-38 • The Red Ones

Do you not say, "There are still four months and then comes the harvest? Behold, I say to you, lift up your eyes and look at the fields, for they are already white for harvest!
John 4:34

As a result of the Samaritan woman's testimony, crowds of people were on their way to Jesus from her town to meet him. He described them to the disciples as a *white harvest*. And right away, it's clear that Jesus sees the harvest of souls differently than most of us do.

When we think about the people in the circles of our lives' influence coming to faith, we think of it as a future event – something we're still working toward. We're still planting, watering, feeding, and pruning. There's work to be done. But according to Jesus, the harvest is now.

One day, I was with one of my grandsons. He was almost three at the time. And I asked him to show me the vegetable garden he helped his other set of grandparents plant in a fenced off part of their property. So, we were on our way walking there.

As we got closer, I could see the rows of vegetables and flowers. And even though we weren't close enough for me to see the signs that indicated which variety was which, I could recognize the tomato plants. I could see that there were a lot of green tomatoes. And I noted that there was going to be a sizeable harvest in the near future but the fruit wasn't ready yet.

Just then, my grandson – who'd been walking right by my side – took off like a bolt of lightning and ran for those tomato plants. And before I knew it, he'd grabbed the only red, ripe tomato in the bunch, pulled it off the plant, and ate it in about three bites.

I was stunned. I thought, "Did I just witness my grandson eat a tomato of his own free will?" Then, after I got over that minor shock, I realized I hadn't even seen the red tomato.

But that's the only one my grandson saw.

I think when Jesus surveys the planting of his gospel garden, he tends to focus on the red ones. I want to do more of that too.

4:39-42 • It's Got to be Personal

Then they said to the woman, "Now we believe, not because of what you said, for we ourselves have heard Him and we know that this is indeed the Christ, the Savior of the world."
John 4:42

John 4:39 says that many people from the city of Sychar became believers because of the testimony of the Samaritan woman. And, hallelujah, may we all have that kind of gospel impact on our communities. But verse 42 clarifies that the real reason they came to place their faith in Jesus was because they met him personally.

And that makes me think about the tendency of Christians that's as old as the church itself to insert a layer of *celebrity* ministers or *professional* Christians into a space between us and Jesus. Here's what I mean.

I think all of us know what it's like to be deeply impacted by the ministry of a great Christian leader, speaker, teacher, pastor, writer, or worship musician. And that's wonderful unless the result is that we start allowing our relationship with Jesus to be *through* them.

When I watch a movie, I experience a story *through* the talent and skill of professionals – actors, writers, directors, camera operators, etc. But I can't let my Christian life become like that where I'm experiencing the unfolding story of my relationship with Jesus *through* the talent, skill, or even the calling and anointing of anyone else. It's got to be *personal*.

May our lives be richly blessed by the devotion of prominent and influential Christian leaders. But let's make sure to have a first-person, real-time relationship with Jesus today.

4:43-45 • He is More Than...

For Jesus Himself testified that a prophet has no honor in his own country.
John 4:44

A fter Jesus spent a couple of days with the Samaritans, he continued his journey northward to his home *region*. But, there's a glaring omission in the passage that describes this. It says he returned to his home *region* of Galilee, but it doesn't say he went to his home *town* of Nazareth. However, we *are* told why he may have chosen not to go to there.

The Lord said that a prophet is not honored in his *own country*. And that phrase, *own country*, is used in the Gospels of Matthew and Mark specifically as a reference to Nazareth. In those passages, we're told that Jesus didn't perform many miracles there because of the unbelief of the people. And we're also told that their unbelief was specifically due to their inability to accept that Jesus was more than just the local carpenter's son – Mary's boy, the kid down the street. Their expectations of him were small because they had a limited definition of him.

Their constrained view of him didn't limit his power. But it did limit their ability to benefit from it.

I love to vacation in Hawaii. And I've been going there at least once a year since 1996. That's when I made my first trip to the islands to speak in a conference. And I fell in love – with the people, the culture, the music, the pace, the climate, and the natural beauty. Most importantly, I found that of all the places I've been in this world, Hawaii is a place where I can truly rest. I'm not exactly sure why – and it may all be just in my head – but it's become very important to me for that reason.

But for the first 40 years of my life, I didn't benefit from all that. And it was specifically because of my limited definition of

Hawaii. I considered it a place for surfers and sun-bathers. And since I'm neither, I couldn't imagine why I would I want to go there.

So, I'm deeply grateful to God for arranging for me to have my definition of Hawaii expanded so I could receive the blessing those Islands have been to me.

And that makes me wonder, have I defined Jesus in a small, narrow, or constrained way that limits my ability to benefit from all he wants to do in my life? And the answer is, of course I have. The magnitude of our Savior is beyond description. So, any way I imagine him is less than he truly is. But that doesn't mean I can't have my awareness of his greatness expanded. And that's my goal for today. Jesus, help me embrace more of who you are.

4:46-54 • Three Types of Faith

So the man believed the word that Jesus spoke to him, and he went his way.

John 4:50b

C hapter four concludes with the record of Jesus healing the nobleman's son. And among other things, it teaches us a very important lesson about faith.

There are actually three types of faith on display in this passage.

The first is what I call, *what-have-I-got-to-lose?* faith. And it's based on what Jesus *might do*. It's the kind of faith the nobleman exercised when he traveled all the way from Capernaum to Cana to see if Jesus could help his dying son. And it's the kind of faith that often motivates our desperate prayers for help when we find ourselves facing challenging circumstances. It's not very deeply rooted, but it is a form of faith most of us can relate to.

Another of the kinds of faith on display in this account is what I call, *what-an-amazing-God-we-have!* faith. And it's based on what Jesus *has done*. It's the kind of faith described in verse 53 and experienced by the nobleman after receiving the news that his son had been healed. This is the kind of exultant, shout-it-from-the-rooftop faith we all hope to experience as we rejoice in the answer to a prayer. It's an easy kind of faith that erupts unbidden from our grateful hearts.

And all of us hope that we will be able to jump directly from *what-have-I-got-to-lose?* faith to *what-an-amazing-God-we-have!* faith. We want our desperate cries to God to always result in immediate and triumphant answers to prayer.

But most of the time, a third type of faith needs to be exercised in the space between the other two. I call it, *what-am-I-going-to-do?* faith. And it's based on what Jesus *has said*. It's the kind of faith the nobleman exercised when he chose to obey the Lord's command to return home trusting what Jesus said about his son having been healed. This is a much more mature faith and demands more of us spiritually. But it's the kind of faith God is always seeking to develop in us when we face life's trials.

I can't know what types of challenges you're facing today. But I do know they provide you with an opportunity to hold tightly to God's word, trust it, act on it, and discover what an amazing God we have!

CHAPTER FIVE

5:1-5 • Alive but not Really Living

Now a certain man was there who had an infirmity thirty-eight years.
John 5:5

In the first section of chapter 5, we have the record of Jesus healing a man at the pool of Bethesda. In the setup, we're told that Jesus was in Jerusalem to attend one of the Jewish feasts, and that while he was there, he visited a pool where sick people were brought hoping to be healed by its waters.

A large number of people with a variety of illnesses were perpetually gathered there waiting for the water to be stirred up. They believed that if they were the first into the pool following one of these stirrings, they would be healed.

We're also told that this periodic movement of the water was caused by the action of an angel. But please note that it does *not* say God was behind this. In fact, there's nothing in either the testimony of the Bible or the ministry of Jesus to support the idea we have a God who toys with people like that.

On the other hand, that's exactly the kind of thing Satan would do. And I think it's clear that this was a situation where the devil was cruelly exploiting people's superstitions by preying on their desperation.

The Greek word translated here as *angel* simply means *messenger*. But the Bible uses it for both God's angelic messengers and Satan's demons. It's the context of the specific Scripture passage that clarifies which one is meant. And I think that based on what I've already said, the word is used here to describe demonic action.

I think it's highly likely that somewhere in the history of this place a mythology began to develop about its healing qualities. There are many places that have a similar healing mythology even in our world today. And they attract people who have no other hope. I think the waters of Bethesda would periodically be stirred up by demons just to keep this false hope alive to torment people.

Now with that understanding as the background, we're introduced in verse 5 to a man Jesus is going to heal. And what I'd like you to consider as we begin an examination of this event in Jesus' ministry, is that this man is clearly not dying. He's been sick for 38 years. But more importantly, he's not really living either. And I have a feeling you may be able to relate to that. I know I can.

I know what it's like to be alive but not really living – not experiencing the life Jesus meant for me. And if that sounds familiar to you too, get ready. The passage before us is going to reveal how we can see our Savior turn that around. And I invite you to explore it with me.

5:6-8 • Rise

He said to him, "Do you want to be made well?"
John 5:6b

J esus approached a man who'd been sick for 38 years – not really dying, but not really living either. He'd apparently spent his entire life in a condition of brokenness and the Lord asked if he'd like to be made well.

The Greek phrase translated here as *be made well* communicates the idea of being restored to the intended state or made whole. And I think the offer of complete restoration implied in that simple question is just astounding to consider.

What's even more amazing is to realize this is exactly the same offer Jesus makes to each of us. He steps onto the scene of our life's devastation, looks us in the eye, and asks us if we want to be restored to our intended state. Dear God! How amazing is his love!

But look at the man's reply. He'd been asked a yes or no question. But he didn't answer with a simple, yes. He answered with an excuse for remaining in his brokenness and offered an explanation for why he couldn't be healed.

O my goodness! Is that like us or what?

He told Jesus that there were conditions and circumstances sourced outside himself that prevented him from being healed. He described the fact that since he couldn't walk and didn't have anyone to help him, he couldn't get into the moving water fast enough and someone else always got there first.

And isn't that how we often respond to our Savior's offer of restoration? We say things like, "I can never be whole because of what my father did to me. I can't live the life I was made for because I never received the educational opportunities others have, because I don't have enough money, because I have this disability, because this or that agency, organization, government, or person failed me." And our list goes on and on.

But Jesus was still standing there asking a simple yes or no question – "Do you want to be made well?" And in spite of the man's all-too-human response, Jesus offered him three steps to recovery. The first of these was, *rise.*

He was asking the man to stop excusing himself and simply receive the healing being offered. And I believe some of you may be hearing the same thing from your Savior right now.

I know it sounds like he's asking you to do something impossible. And it is…for you. But *not* for him. Stop making excuses for your brokenness or blaming it on someone or something outside yourself. Take his hand right now and *rise.*

5:8 • Take up Your Bed

Jesus said to him, "Rise, take up your bed and walk."
John 5:8

Let's continue our consideration of Jesus' healing of the man at the pool of Bethesda. And let's remember that after 38 years of sickness, this man was clearly not dying, but he wasn't really living either. So, Jesus entered the scene of his brokenness, and in the form of a simple question, offered him the opportunity to be restored to his intended state.

Then, the Lord gave him three steps to wholeness. And the first of those was to *rise*, which we discussed last time.

After that, Jesus said, "take up your bed." In other words, he told him that if he wanted to experience true healing, he was going to have to pack up his campsite.

For many years now, I've enjoyed watching a reality TV show called *Survivor*. The contestants try to avoid being eliminated from the game until there are only three players left. Then, those who've been forced to leave vote for a winner from the three survivors. But before that vote, the final players will almost always burn down the camp they've been living in. And they do that as a dramatic statement of the fact that they will not be coming back.

Something very similar is embedded in the Lord's statement here. He was telling the man that if he was going to actually live in the healing being offered, he would have to eliminate the possibility of coming back to Bethesda.

Why is this important? Because we all prefer the security of a *known* past – even if it's uncomfortable – over the uncertainties of an *unknown* future. And for this man who'd been sick his entire life, a future of wholeness – as desirable as it may be – was filled with uncertainties. So, unless he removed the possibility, in those times when his healing would be challenged, he would be vulnerable to the temptation to return to the twisted familiarity of what he knew.

Now there's also the issue of identity. I think it's clear by what this man said to Jesus that he had come to see himself through the lens of his unhealth and had begun to define himself by it. There's a huge difference between someone thinking of themselves as a person who *has* a struggle with alcohol and as someone who *is* an alcoholic. And the devil has a lot of expertise in exploiting our issues and convincing us to label ourselves by them. But that makes us less available to healing.

In a sense, Jesus was telling the man that as long as he had his sick bed to go back to, he would be vulnerable to the temptation to think of himself as sick instead of as a man who had an illness but is now whole.

On top of that, every form of human brokenness has a support structure that's been built around it – friends and family who enable the unhealth, habits that have developed, distorted assumptions, etc. And unless that structure is dismantled, the gravitational pull backward can be overwhelming. For instance, if a person is freed by Jesus from a pornography addiction, unless that person is also willing to tear down their well-worn pathways for accessing porn, it will be too easy to slide back into the familiar.

So, we have before us a critical component in the process of healing Jesus wants to bring to your life and mine. Just like the man at the pool, he's asking if we want to be made whole. If so, he says it will *require* us to be ruthless about cutting off every route back to brokenness.

Are you ready to take up your bed? Jesus is with you right now and ready to give you the clarity, courage, and confidence you need to do it.

5:9-15 • Walk

And immediately the man was made well, took up his bed, and walked.

John 5:9a

We've been considering the account of the man at the Pool of Bethesda. Remember, this was a man who had been sick for thirty-eight years – not really dying, but not really living either. Then, just like he does for each of us, Jesus showed up with an invitation for him to trade his brokenness for wholeness. But he said the restoration process would require three things – to *rise, take up your bed,* and after that, *walk.*

After having previously looked at the first two of these, let's zero in on the last one and what it means for anyone who wants to receive Christ's gift of wholeness and begin to truly live.

There are a couple of things I'd like to focus on. To start with, Jesus was inviting the man to choose to literally step forward into the rest of his life – the life he was made for. But why would he even have to say this? Because it doesn't come naturally.

Although the passage doesn't say so explicitly, it clearly implies that this man had never walked before. And we've already talked about the human tendency to prefer a known past to an unknown future. So, let's not miss the point that living in wholeness is a moment-by-moment choice to do the impossible – to defy gravity in the power of the Spirit. Like the man at the pool, it's not something any of us has ever done before. And we simply don't know how.

But Jesus made it clear that it's just like walking – putting one foot in front of the other – taking one step at time. It's not about arriving somewhere. It's about starting a journey, one that involves discovery, development, and delight with every footfall.

And we cannot afford to skip even one of them. Even when the route isn't a straight line, we don't have to figure out where it leads. All we have to do is keep our eyes on Jesus and *walk*. He can be trusted with everything else.

But there's another thing.

As the man from the pool began to move forward in his healing, he was immediately confronted by the Jewish leaders telling him he was breaking their religious law by carrying his bed on the Sabbath. And that's exactly the kind of thing that happens to everyone who chooses to step across the threshold from brokenness to wholeness. Our healing will be challenged, and ferociously, because the devil cannot afford to have God's people actually living in wholeness. It poses such a threat to his strategies that he is always quick and loud with his opposition.

Should that make us afraid? No! The Bible says that the battle is the Lord's (1 Samuel 17:47) not ours, and he's already won it (John 19:30). So even when the enemy roars at us with his temptations, condemnations, and accusations, all we need to do is *walk* – right past him one step after another into the glorious life Christ is releasing us into.

And I love the fact that as the formerly-sick-but-now-healed man shouldered his way past his accusers choosing to obey his healer rather than surrender to their threats, he ran right into Jesus who was there to meet him in the Temple on the other side of that opposition.

I believe that will be true for you too. No matter what may challenge your wholeness today, just take one step at a time and *walk* right by, through, or over it. You'll find that Jesus is on the other side.

5:16 • The Spirit of Control

*For this reason the Jews persecuted Jesus, and sought to kill Him,
because He had done these things on the Sabbath.*
John 5:16

In this verse, we're told flatly that the Jewish religious elite wanted to kill Jesus. And we're also told why. It was because he had healed a sick man on the Sabbath.

Now, let me get this straight. The *religious* leaders wanted to *kill* Jesus because he chose the wrong day of the week on which to *heal* a man who'd been sick for 38 years. What am I missing here?

I know Sabbath-keeping is an important thing with God. You can't read past the second chapter in the Bible without discovering that he's so serious about it he personally modeled it. But it's also clear that God meant Sabbath to be a blessing to us not a curse. In fact, Jesus said (Mark 2:27), "The Sabbath was made for man, and not man for the Sabbath."

God gave us the gift of one day out of every seven set aside purely for spiritual renewal, physical rest, relational restoration, emotional recovery, and intellectual recalibration.

So, how did something so good for us become so twisted?

Well, like everything religionists get their hands on, Sabbath had been embellished with layer upon layer of regulations God never intended. And they exploited these rules as a means of exercising control over people. And that's the key word, *control.*

That kind of control is a bad thing, and Jesus will always be a threat to it. I know because he came after it in my life.

Please, don't get me wrong. I love my birth family. But all families have some measure of dysfunction, and one of the symptoms of ours was that we could never seem to get anywhere on time. And I clearly remember being dropped off late again for baseball practice one day when I was about nine years old. As I walked to the field knowing I would have to apologize to my coach and teammates again for being late, I remember saying to myself, "When I have *control*, I will never be late again!"

And that vow set in motion decades of drivenness and controlling behavior that eventually would bring me to the brink of losing my marriage, family, health, and ministry had not my loving Lord squared off against it in my life. All those years before, I had given place to something that was ruining me along with everything and everyone I loved. The control I had become so proud of exercising was really a spirit that was controlling me.

It's a long, but beautiful story how Jesus confronted and set me free from the spirit of control that I won't take the time now to tell. But if the little I've said sounds at all familiar to your own life, please don't wait another minute. Come in prayer with humble repentance to the one who is ready to release you from this bondage. Invite the Lord of the Sabbath to bring rest to your soul.

5:17 • He's Never Off the Job

But Jesus answered them, "My Father has been working until now,
and I have been working."
John 5:17

T he Jewish religious leaders had determined that Jesus deserved the death penalty because he healed a man on the Sabbath. And the Lord responded by making two things clear. One, that he is the Son of God. And two, that he was only doing what his Father has been and continues doing – working.

Yes, Genesis – the first book of the Bible – tells us that God rested on the seventh day. And no, Jesus wasn't undermining the example God was setting by that or the commands and vital principals of Sabbath-keeping. But he was stating the obvious – that on the seventh day, God rested from his creation work, but not from being the God whose ongoing activity sustains all things.

In other words, Jesus was reminding them that the throne of God is not a lounge chair.

And in doing so, he was silencing the lie that God is somehow disconnected, unconcerned, or uninvolved with us. Contrary to those who imagine God like a divine watchmaker who wound up his creation, let it go, and then moved on to another project, Jesus was describing God as intensely engaged with his universe. And it's clear from the context, that he meant for us to understand God never ceases to be interested in, involved with, and engaged with us.

The other day, I walked by a construction project. New homes are being built in my neighborhood. But at the time I was strolling by, none of the workers were on the job. They'd all gone home after putting in their day's labor.

God is not like that. He's never off the job.

106

I know — because I'm a target of the devil's lies just like you — that we can frequently be subjected to the temptation to feel like God has abandoned us or at least has temporarily lost interest in what we're facing or going through. But that's not the truth, and that's exactly why this verse is so important to hang on to.

Our Savior stood up in the face of the murderous persecution of the Scribes and Pharisees to emphatically declare that no matter what, he is continually and purposefully working on our behalf. Let's allow that assurance to dispel every shadow of doubt about our Savior's presence and engagement with us today.

5:18-23 • An Exact Reflection

...The Son can do nothing of Himself, but what He sees the Father do; for whatever He does, the Son also does in like manner.
John 5:19b

I'm not sure how it's possible to become even more angry with someone after you've reached the point of wanting to kill them, but that's the state of outrageous agitation the religious leaders had reached regarding Jesus. They had already issued a death sentence for his healing of a sick man on the Sabbath. But this passage informs us that they were even more ticked off at his clear claim of equality with God.

And Jesus refused to back down from this. He declared in no uncertain terms that everything he did and said was an exact reflection of the Heavenly Father and that he should be honored in the same way the Father is.

And there you have it. That's why the Jewish elite was so mad. It was impossible for them to remain ambivalent about the question of who Jesus was. The testimony of his life was crowding them toward a decision point – one they were violently resisting. To embrace the truth of his divinity would have required that they surrender to his Lordship. And that's what made their blood boil.

However, for the rest of us, there's wonderful news here. Jesus is God! Everything the Gospels reveal about Jesus that moves us to fall so deeply in love with him is exactly true of the Father as well. There is no difference. And this is incredibly important and healing on many levels, especially for those who have trouble relating to the Heavenly Father because of the failures of their earthly ones.

As someone who has spent my life caring for the wounded souls of people, I've seen first-hand the damage a dad can do by his words and deeds even if unintentional. The devil loves to exploit a man's brokenness to inflict painful scars on his children and thereby cause them to recoil from the love of God. What better way for Satan to keep someone imprisoned in their hurt than to emotionally cut them off from the only one who can free them.

But Jesus is the answer. He put on display the father-heart of God. The closer we examine his life, the more we see what God is really like and the more any barriers melt away.

So, if you've been victimized by this strategy of the enemy to prevent you from experiencing the healing embrace of the lover of your soul, let me stand with you today as you welcome the Son to introduce you to the Father.

5:24 • Put Your Butt in the Seat

Most assuredly, I say to you, he who hears My word and believes in Him who sent Me has everlasting life, and shall not come into judgment, but has passed from death into life.
John 5:24

After emphatically declaring to the Jewish leaders that he is co-equal with the Heavenly Father, Jesus went on to say that for anyone who responds to his message by believing in the Father, three things become true: something has *already* happened, something will *never* happen, and something is happening *right now*. But before we look a little closer at these, let's make sure we understand what he meant by believing in the Father.

The Greek word translated as *believes* in this verse is a word that conveys more than just concluding that the design of a chair, for instance, could support your weight. This word is about the action that flows from that conclusion and results in actually putting your butt in the seat. It's about trust, and trust that results in commitment.

Jesus was calling these leaders, everyone overhearing that conversation, and all who've heard these words since to take action on what they heard and place the full weight of their faith on him. And if that describes you, I've got some excellent news.

First, you have *already* – as Jesus said – "passed from death into life." The spiritual death that was the result of your sin is now behind you – forgiven, cleansed, covered – and up ahead as far as you can see is the gift of life that God gives his kids.

Second, you will *never* experience judgment, not now, or at any time in the future. No matter how hard the devil may try to bring you under condemnation, that shame no longer has your name on it (Romans 8:1).

And third, you are living in the stream of "everlasting life" *right now*. And Jesus wasn't just talking about its duration – how long it lasts. He was talking about the type of life it is. This verse employs the Greek word *zoe* which the New Testament uses to describe the kind of life God has – deeper, richer in every way than mere existence or anything this world can offer.

All of this is yours as a result of your faith in Christ. Live every minute of this day in the awareness of that.

Oh! And if by chance you haven't yet become a believer, what are you waiting for? Put your butt in the seat.

5:25-26 • Spiritual CPR

For as the Father has life in Himself, so He has granted the Son to have life in Himself...
John 5:26

In this passage, Jesus began to describe something happening at that very moment that will also happen at a time yet to come. He was talking about dead people coming to life. And he started by saying the Hebrew word *amen* twice. This is sometimes translated as, "verily, verily" or "truly, truly," or "most assuredly." And the Lord uses this introduction method 25 different times in John's Gospel when he wants to underscore what follows. It's as though he's saying, "There's nothing more true than this." In other words, he wants us to pay very close attention to what he's about to say.

I'll wait until we get to verse 28 to look at the implications of this passage on what he described as "the hour that is coming." But for now, I'd like to explore its impact on what he calls the hour that "now is."

Jesus was saying that right now the dead who hear his voice will live. And yes, every time the Bible tell us about Jesus raising a physically dead person to life he's described as speaking to them first or calling them back to life. But I think it's clear from the context of this passage, that he was referring to those who are spiritually dead being made spiritually alive. And this is possible, he says, because he has "life in himself."

And that's the point.

None of us can engineer our own spiritual resuscitation. Only he's qualified for that job. And that's because he defeated death on the cross and then rose again for us.

Still, many of us try to administer spiritual CPR to ourselves.

There's a hospital located near my home. And CPR or *Cardio*

Pulmonary Resuscitation is a frequent occurrence there. It's a method for attempting to restart someone's heart when they've suffered a cardiac arrest. But you can't do it for yourself. In fact, you can't be more incapable of helping yourself than when you're in that state. It requires someone who *has* life to offer it to the one who *doesn't*.

And when it comes to our spirits, we are completely dependent on Jesus to do that. Not only is spiritual self-help ineffective, it's impossible. None of us can offer life to ourselves.

So, if you long to become fully alive, let me tenderly invite you to stop the insanity of trying to do it yourself. Instead, just respond to the voice of the one calling you to life.

5:27-29 • The Resurrection of Life

...For the hour is coming in which all who are in the graves will hear His voice and come forth — those who have done good, to the resurrection of life, and those who have done evil, to the resurrection of condemnation.

John 5:28b-29

In this section, Jesus described his role as our judge.

He referred to himself in the preceding two verses (John 5:25-26) as the *Son of God* who can – right now – offer spiritual life to those who are dead in their sins if they will simply respond to his voice calling them to faith. But here he described a future occasion when his voice will call all those who have died physically to either a "resurrection of life" or a "resurrection of condemnation." And he said his authority to execute this judgment is on the basis of what the Father has given him as the *Son of Man*. This change in title is worth noting.

Jesus is both Son of God and Son of Man. He is fully divine and fully human. And this is what uniquely qualifies him to be both eternal-life-giver, and judge. As Son of God, he personally paid the penalty for our sin so we could have the payment of his suffering and death applied to our record by faith. And as Son of Man, he victoriously stared down every kind of temptation and has first-hand knowledge of every form of human experience so that he alone has the righteous authority to be our judge.

So, when those who have refused to receive his offer of salvation during their lifetimes stand before him on that future day of judgment, there will be no excuse, no alibi, no defense. But if you're reading this, that doesn't have to be your story.

In verse 29, there's a very wonderful and hope-filled use of two different Greek words that are translated in the New King

James Version of the Bible by the same English word, *done*. Jesus said that the resurrections of life and condemnation are the result of having *done* good or *done* evil. But he's not saying that a person's eternal destiny is based on whether or not they've racked up sufficient good-works points (Ephesian 2:8-9).

The word translated, *done*, in the first instance describes a one-time act. In the second, the word is about something habitually *done*. The Lord is saying that with one act – placing our faith in his saving grace – we can ensure our "resurrection of life" and wipe out the consequences of having *habitually* turned our backs on him.

Now that's good news! If you haven't yet, receive it. And if you have, share it.

5:30 • Judging Others

I can of Myself do nothing. As I hear, I judge; and My judgment is righteous, because I do not seek My own will but the will of the Father who sent Me.

John 5:30b

Jesus said his assignment as divine judge – which he described in the preceding verses – is administered solely on the basis of instructions he receives from the Father. And in that context, he made this incredible statement, *"I can of Myself do nothing."*

Now of course, as God incarnate, Jesus possessed everything required – authority, power, wisdom, knowledge – to do anything. But he made clear that in his role as our judge, he specifically and purposefully chose not to act independent of the Father. Philippians 2:5-11 describes his submission in detail and declares it to be the reason that ultimately every knee will bow and tongue confess he is Lord.

So, Jesus' words here are extremely significant. And I think that's especially true of the last half of the verse where he said that because he seeks the will of the Father and not his own, his judgment is righteous.

That forces me to consider how I judge other people.

Every day, I pass judgment on those I hear, see, meet, and interact with. I can't help it. And neither can you. We're instinctively wired to evaluate others on the fly. Have you ever heard a stranger's voice on a podcast, radio show, or phone call and determined what their appearance, personality, and motivation must be like even though you've never seen or met them? We all do that. It's a human trait that I suppose is a form of self-protection. But I'll bet you've noticed that it's almost never accurate.

The prejudgments I make of people almost always turn out

116

to be wrong once I actually get to know them. And if you've ever been unfairly judged yourself, you know it feels terrible and is often very hard to change.

I once rented a home from a guy who – for some unknown reason – just decided he didn't like me. And nothing I did to try and change his mind was ever successful. He just doggedly clung to his false initial impression of me no matter what, and I could not overcome his skepticism and mistrust. So, I eventually had to move out.

I don't want to do that to others. But I do. Like the obviously homeless woman I passed on the street the other day. Based on her appearance alone, I created an entire profile of her in my mind. And a pretty negative one I must add. How unfair was that? So, a few minutes later, when I realized what I'd done, I had to confess my sin to God and repent of it.

I'd like to discover a better – more righteous – way to handle this aspect of life. And, as always, Jesus points the way.

He said the key to righteous judgment is seeking God's will not my own. In other words, if I will simply start choosing to see others through the lens of his desires for them instead of through my own fears and prejudices, my perspective will become more like his. I want to do that, don't you? And what a better world this would be if everyone did!

5:31-32 • Case Closed

There is another who bears witness of Me...
John 5:32a

In the final section of chapter 5, a kind of courtroom drama played out. Jesus – like a skillful defense attorney presenting his final argument before the Jewish religious leaders – detailed the weighty testimonial evidence for his claim to be the Son of God.

He began by acknowledging that according to their law – requiring two independent witnesses to establish the truth of a matter – serving as his own witness would be insufficient. That's what he meant when he said, "My witness is not true." He didn't mean he was lying. He was simply agreeing that under their system, his personal testimony alone would not be enough.

So, over the remainder of the chapter, he reminded them of the powerful testimony they'd already heard from not just two, but four witnesses. And in verse 32, before elaborating in detail later in the passage, he teased them with some of what was coming when he said, "There is another who bears witness of me." A clear and unequivocal reference to God, the Father.

And reading those words again today caused my throat to tighten with emotion and my eyes to tear up as I was reminded of the forceful impact of the testimony of my Heavenly Father in the recurring case of the devil's suit against my salvation. It seems that almost daily Satan attempts to call into question my right to consider myself a child of God. And he skillfully introduces as evidence all the dirt he continues digging up from the remains of my sinfulness.

And it can be very convincing. When the fruits of my wickedness are paraded through the courtroom of my soul, I can often find my personal witness to God's grace losing ground against the testimony of my sinful past.

But God has declared in John 1:12 that because I have placed my faith in Jesus, I have been given legal standing as a child of God. And Romans 8:16 says, "The Spirit Himself bears witness with our spirit that we are children of God."

So, if you find yourself today being tempted by the accuser to doubt your place in God's family because of something he dredged up from your past, remember 1 John 1:9. "If we confess our sins, He is faithful and just to forgive us our sins, and to cleanse us from all unrighteousness."

Case closed.

5:33-47 • Willing to Come

But you were not willing to come to Me that you may have life.
John 5:40

Jesus concluded the argument he was making to the religious leaders regarding his claim to be the Son of God by identifying four witnesses that had already testified on his behalf: John the Baptist, the miracles he performed, God the Father, and the Old Testament Scriptures.

For those who resisted breaking with the pack to embrace his lordship, Jesus reminded them that none other than the much-respected John the Baptist had publicly declared him the Son of God, staking his own reputation on the truth of that statement.

For those who refused to believe without tangible proof, he reminded them that they had seen his miracles with their own eyes.

For those who were stubbornly withholding faith unless the heavens opened and they heard God speak in an audible voice, he reminded them that they had been personally present as that exact thing happened when he was baptized by John.

For those who were clinging to their skepticism until there was theological agreement on the subject, he pointed out that the Holy Scriptures speak clearly of him and affirm his divinity throughout.

And that brings us to verse 40 where Jesus said that placing faith in him for salvation – or anything else for that matter – is really never about convincing arguments, proofs, and evidence no matter what anyone says. It's always about a *willingness* to trust him. And Jesus promises here that this simple act of surrender is what opens the door to the life we long for. So, why are people, including you and me, so often *unwilling*?

Well, I'll just speak for myself. Taking any step of faith, requires that I confront the desire of my sinful nature to maintain control. But faith is the exact opposite of control, isn't it? Trusting Jesus with my health, finances, marriage, career – let alone my eternal destiny – means being willing to release the control of those things to him, believing there is no better place for them than in his hands.

But that's the issue, right? Do we really believe that?

It's hard for me to admit this in the face of the overwhelming evidence of my Lord's love, faithfulness, and power. He has never failed me. Still, there are times I hesitate to trust my cares to him. And perhaps that's true for you too.

If so, let's agree today, to come to him *willingly,* releasing all our concerns to him that we may know life as he intends.

The John Project

CHAPTER SIX

6:1-4 • There's Always a Backstory

After these things Jesus went over the Sea of Galilee...
John 6:1a

T he first part of chapter 6 tells us about the time when Jesus fed thousands of people with only five loaves and two fish. And the first four verses set up the story by giving us the time of year and the location where it happened. We're told it was springtime just before Passover and in a deserted area across the Sea of Galilee.

But before going any further, I'd like to focus on just the first three words in verse one, "After these things…" Why? Because there's always a backstory. And this lets us know there's a context for what follows.

By prefacing his account with this phrase, John let us know there's even more to the story and implied that we should consider these additional details. He made it clear they're worth digging for.

And we don't have to search far. The other three Gospels – especially Mark – fill in the six-month gap between John chapters five and six. And we find out there was a reason Jesus had taken his disciples across the lake. He was leading them to a wilderness area for some rest.

They were all dealing with the emotional impact of John the Baptist being beheaded by Herod. The disciples had just returned from their first ministry tours and needed debriefing. And the intensifying of Jesus's miracle ministry had created so much activity we're told they didn't even have time to eat.

So that's why they crossed the lake. And it makes a difference to know that, doesn't it?

In a very crude way, it's like the sign nailed to a big tree near my home. Unless you take the time to stop and read it, you probably wouldn't give this tree a second thought. But if you do, you find out that it was brought here by a sea captain from a distant port and planted more than 150 years ago. There's a backstory. And digging for it makes a difference in how you see the tree.

And that's true for people too. There's always a backstory.

But we usually interact with others based on the superficial. We rarely stop to even think that there may be more to consider.

And this is especially true for how we relate to ourselves. We waste so much of our emotional resources focused on our surface issues instead of asking Jesus, "What's the backstory here?" But if we did, we'd be much more likely to discover the context for what he's trying to deal with in our lives and be better able to cooperate with him as he brings us healing and deliverance.

So, I encourage you today. When you find yourself wrestling with the *stuff* in your life – and you know what I mean – ask the Lord to help you see the backstory. Stop ignoring the real issues while whining about what you think God should be doing to help you but isn't. Be willing instead to stop and read the signs that reveal how these things got rooted in your life in the first place. Then, you'll be better able to allow the Lord to set you up for what comes "after these things."

6:5-6 • The Outcome is Never in Doubt

But this He said to test him, for He Himself knew what He would do.

John 6:6

The loaves and fish narrative opens by describing a massive crowd of 5,000 men plus women and children that was approaching. And when Jesus saw the multitude, he asked one of the disciples how they were going to feed all of them.

Then, verse 6 reveals two very important things we should remember whenever we encounter a need that has the potential to overwhelm us, whether it's spiritual, physical, financial, or relational.

First, we're told the Lord was using this as a test. Need always does that – tests our faith. And although these trials can seriously rock our world and challenge us to our core, God's purpose in allowing them is never to disqualify or defeat us. It's always to reveal both how far he's already brought us and to expose areas of trust he wants to help us grow into.

It's like the gym that a friend of mine manages. All day, people walk through his doors determined to put their bodies to the test. They pay my friend's company for the opportunity to be challenged with weights, machines, and instructors for the benefit of seeing their health, strength and fitness increase.

In the same way, the Bible tells us to rejoice when our faith is tested because it's increasing our spiritual health (1 Peter 1:6). God is using it for our good.

The second thing verse 6 tells us is that Jesus knew in advance what he was going to do. The outcome was never in doubt. God is in control. As believers, these what-in-the-world-am-I-going-to-do kind of situations always reach us through the filter of God's love, mercy, and grace. We square off against them in an environment managed by the power of the sovereign God. As his kids, we are never – and I repeat, never – in jeopardy.

I can't know what kind of need may be testing your faith today, but Jesus does. And as challenging as it may seem, remember these soul-securing truths. One, if you let him, your Savior will use it to strengthen your faith muscles. And two, Jesus already has a rock-solid plan for meeting that need.

Trust him!

6:7-9 • The Faith of a Child

There is a lad here who has five barley loaves and two small fish...
John 6:9a

W e've already discussed how Jesus used a need – the hunger of thousands – to test faith. We learned that when God allows our faith to be challenged, his purpose is to increase our spiritual health not deplete it. And we also learned that our Lord is always in control of a trial's outcome. He can be fully trusted.

Now, verses 7 through 9 reveal three different types of response to this test of faith. Let's see if we can find ourselves in them, and by comparing, discover a better way to handle the faith-trials we encounter.

Jesus had posed a question: "How are we going to feed all these people?" And the first response came from Philip. He whipped out his calculator, did the math, and reported to Jesus there was no way they could afford to buy anywhere close to enough food. He focused on the size of the need and said, "It's too big."

Next up was Andrew. He came to Jesus with five barley loaves and two small fish he'd gotten from a kid who'd brought a lunch with him that day. But then, he asked his own question, "What are they among so many?" You see, he was focused on himself and was saying, "I don't have enough."

But there's another person involved in this episode, the boy with the lunch. And although the text doesn't specifically say so, it clearly implies that this young man freely offered his loaves and fish. They weren't taken from him, they were given. And by doing so, he was demonstrating that he was focused on Jesus, and by his actions, saying, "I believe you can do anything."

Oh, the faith of a child!

Dear Lord, when I next face a need that tests my faith, may my response be the simple childlike trust demonstrated by that young man. May my choice be not to focus on the size of the need or my own limited resources to meet it. Help me instead to trust in the greatness of who you are. May my heart's cry be, "You can do anything!"

6:10 • Obedience Paves the Way

Then Jesus said, "Make the people sit down."...So the men sat down,
in number about five thousand.
John 6:10

As he moved toward the miraculous feeding of the crowd, Jesus asked his disciples to instruct the people to be seated in the grassy field. And Mark's gospel gives us the additional information that Jesus wanted the people to be seated in groups of fifties and hundreds. Mark also takes the time to specifically tell us that they did as instructed.

John chapter 6 verse 10 is easy to skip over on our way to the main event. But there's no filler in the Bible. God never wastes words. And the importance of the principle contained here cannot be overstated. Jesus was setting the stage for a miracle. And if you think you might ever need one of those, pay attention.

He was preparing for the organized distribution of a large quantity of food. He was about to supernaturally multiply five loaves and two fish to feed 5,000 men plus women and children. But he was the only one who knew that. No one else there that day had any idea what was about to happen.

Just stop and think about that. The disciples and the hungry crowd obeyed Jesus without even the slightest understanding of why he was asking or how their compliance could have anything to do with the meeting of their need.

And that's the point. They did what he said simply because he said it. That's what faith is all about: trust-filled obedience. And displays of God's miraculous power are nearly always preceded by an act of faith that rarely seems to be relevant to the need. Like when Jesus directed the servants at the wedding in Cana to fill six pots with water and take a sample to the master of the feast. They could never have guessed the water would become wine. But their simple obedience facilitated an amazing miracle.

Or like the time I responded to a very vague prompting I thought might be from the Lord. I was just folding the laundry at home one day when I sensed he was asking me to reach out to a young couple I'd heard about but hadn't yet met and ask if they'd be interested in allowing me to mentor them in ministry. There was no way I could have known the miracle Jesus was setting up. At that time, I had no idea that my wife and I would soon be embarking on a new season of ministry assignment. And with the small step of obedience I exercised in contacting that couple, the Lord was arranging what became the miraculously smooth transition of pastoral leadership our church experienced when they succeeded us as senior pastors just eighteen months later.

Listen, if you need a miracle today, stop worrying about how in the world God is going to feed the multitudes. Instead, start looking for the nearest divine command you can obey. And if you draw a blank, consider opening the Bible, it's full of them. Your step of child-like obedience – however unrelated it looks like to you – will place in the Lord's hands the raw material he can work with to do something wonderful.

6:11a • The Power of Gratitude

And Jesus took the loaves, and when He had given thanks He
distributed them to the disciples...
John 6:11a

After Jesus had received the loaves and fish from the young man and before those meager provisions became bounty, he gave thanks.

Everything Jesus said and did was intentional, purposeful, and strategic. Among other things, he was modeling for us what a life of faith looks like. So, it's incredibly important to pay close attention to every move he made and every word he spoke.

There's a reason he paused on the way to a miracle of provision to first give thanks. And since I'm often in need of God's supernatural provision, I want to understand why. What was he thankful for? I think it's clear he was thankful for what he'd already been given – five loaves and two fish.

They weren't nearly enough, but Jesus focused on what he'd been given, not on what was still needed. And there's something extremely powerful about that heart-posture that opens the door for the Lord's supernatural supply.

But to be honest, when I'm in need – of money, healing, wisdom, comfort, guidance – gratitude is not usually my response. In fact, quite the opposite. I'm far more likely to complain, express my impatience, and even vent my anger than to be grateful.

But you know what I've found? Thanklessness is habit-forming, and it poisons my soul. So, when God in his faithfulness does supply my need, I'm more likely to think, "Well, it's about time," than to fall on my knees with praise for his goodness. And ultimately, I think that makes me less likely to even recognize the wonderful miracles he regularly performs on my behalf.

I wonder if that might be true for you too. What do you say we choose to survey the circumstances we're in today noting with thankfulness what we've already been given instead of grumbling about what we still need? I wonder how that might change what happens next.

6:11b • Bite-Sized Miracles

He distributed them to the disciples, and the disciples to those sitting down...
John 6:11b

Jesus involved the disciples in the loaves and fish miracle. We're told he distributed the multiplying food to the hungry people through them. The miraculous literally passed through their hands. They were conduits of wonder. I can't even begin to imagine what an amazing experience that must have been.

But as someone who longs to be more useful when God is moving to meet people's needs through displays of his power, I notice two things here that I find extremely helpful.

First, through the preceding events, Jesus made it clear to the disciples that they were not responsible to make the miracle happen. Neither their money nor their culinary skills were involved. It was all Jesus. Their role was to simply dispense what he was creating.

They were like divine delivery-persons. UPS and FedEx drivers aren't required to purchase or manufacture the items in their trucks. Their job is to just make sure the boxes get to the right address, ring the doorbell, and leave them on the porch.

So much pressure comes off when I understand miracles aren't up to me. My job is to lay hands on the sick. It's his to do the healing. My job is to speak the words of prophecy, knowledge, wisdom, and discernment he gives. My job is to pray for the bound and broken-hearted, his is to deliver and comfort.

The second thing I see here is that the grand miracle of feeding the multitude unfolded in stages — mouthful by mouthful. The disciples got to be involved in distributing a series of bite-sized miracles that altogether became something legendary.

Don't misunderstand, a miracle is a miracle. The terms *large* and *small* do not really apply. And God can work massive miracles in an instant. But I've found that for the most part, he invites me to participate in a lot of little ones that accumulate over time into an amazing expression of his glory.

As an older man who has walked with God for a long time now, this is deeply moving to me. I look back over my life and rejoice with amazement at the times I've witnessed demonstrations of God's explosive power. But I also cherish the cumulative weight of all those quieter ones. And I've come to understand the value of living in the daily expectation of a steady stream of God's manifest power.

So, if you're desperate today for a large, loud, and immediate miracle from heaven, we have a God who is more than able. But it may just be that his provision is on the way to your doorstep a box at a time. Don't miss them.

6:12 • Sufficiency and Economy

So when they were filled, He said to His disciples, "Gather up the fragments that remain, so that nothing is lost."
John 6:12

This verse graphically illustrates two important truths about God – he is both lavish and frugal. He is both abundant with his grace and meticulous with his care. Let me explain.

My wife and I are currently remodeling a home. And our contractor is continually asking us if we want this fixture, that color, this window, that door, this tile, or that trim. Frankly, it's wearing us out. But we answer each of his questions with one of our own, "Can we afford it?" We only have so much money.

You know what I mean.

Every resource we have as human beings is finite. We have a limited amount of time, talent, and treasure. And since this is our frame of reference, we tend to imagine God as though he's in the same boat. And even if our theology is better than that, all of us experience times when we hesitate to bring our needs to him because we feel like we may be pushing the limit of what he can afford. But God doesn't have to stretch his supply or budget his benevolence.

The end of verse 11 and the first part of 12 tell us that Jesus didn't stop multiplying the loaves and fish until everyone in the crowd had eaten all they wanted and until they were full. He didn't cheap out. He doesn't have to. He's the maker and master of all things. And when we come to him with our needs, our requests are not evaluated against a limited supply. His gifts of every sort – spiritual, physical, and material – are abundant.

This doesn't license our gluttony. It showcases God's sufficiency. But it's juxtaposed against his economy which is illustrated when he commands the disciples to gather up all the leftovers so that nothing is wasted.

There's clearly a lesson here about our need to exercise better care in how we manage what God gives us. But I think there's even more.

Many of us know what it's like to mourn the ways we have squandered the goodness of God in our pasts. And we imagine that those lost expressions of his love are irretrievable. But our Savior is concerned about discarded fragments. We have a God whose amazing grace is so powerful, he can ensure that nothing of his intentions for us is ultimately forsaken.

Bring your needs to our all-sufficient God and trust him to carefully gather up all the pieces of your life you thought were lost.

6:13-14 • On the Street Where We Live

Then those men, when they had seen the sign that Jesus did, said,
"This is truly the Prophet who is to come into the world."
John 6:14

John 6:13 surveys the aftermath of a miracle. And I'm just mesmerized by the simple statistics. Five loaves and two fish produced twelve baskets of food after filling the bellies of five thousand men plus women and children.

I think we need to take just a few moments to consider the implications of this.

Doesn't it force us to reevaluate our faith? Did Jesus actually do this or not? If he did, how can it be so easy for us to just carry on with the routines of our lives without any expectation that he might want to invade *our* circumstances with his miraculous power?

The next verse says those who had front row seats for that miracle became believers on the spot. So why is it possible for us to read the account of what happened and not be equally moved to belief?

Maybe it has to do with the way we casually read the biblical accounts of miracles as though they're disconnected from our personal reality.

Perhaps I shouldn't admit this, but I'm a bit of a Star Wars nerd. I love watching the Millennium Falcon travel through hyperspace in the films and imagining the lightsaber duals I read about in the books. But I'm well aware that these things only happen "in a galaxy far, far away," not on the street where I live.

So, I have to ask myself, "Is that how I categorize the epic displays of the supernatural I read about in the Bible? Do I intellectually relegate them to another time and place? If so, how do I square that with John 14:12, where Jesus said that after he returned to the Father, those who believe in him would experience even greater works than he performed?

I don't think the Lord could be clearer about his intentions to continue being who he is – the omnipotent God. Everything he does is miraculous – beyond the constraints of this natural world. He can't be any other way. So, let's get our expectations aligned with his attributes in this regard. If we want God to be active on the street where we live, it *will* involve miracles.

So, let's allow Jesus to help us read the Bible differently – to see in its pages not some fantastic story of what happened "once upon a time," but as a preview of what God is prepared to do right now.

6:15 • The Opposite Direction

Therefore when Jesus perceived that they were about to come and take Him by force to make Him king, He departed again to the mountain by Himself alone.

John 6:15

This verse describes Jesus doing something so contrary to my experience, I simply stand in awe. When the crowds were determined to make him their king, he literally walked away. He went the opposite direction – toward solitude and away from the cheers and adoration. In our current season of human history which is so obsessed with celebrity – with the quest for attention, acclaim, and fame at a fever pitch – the Lord's choice here is stunning by contrast.

Now, I need to confess something. A couple of days ago, I posted a Bible study video on my website, podcast, and social media. And over the next twenty-four hours, I caught myself checking for likes and comments every fifteen minutes it seemed. I was behaving like an addict. But once I was able to exercise enough self-control to stop, I began asking God why I craved these *hits* of affirmation so much. And I'm ashamed of the answer.

At first, I tried to convince myself that I was just a little insecure about my identity since recently retiring from being a local church pastor after nearly forty years. Having had such clarity about my life and ministry for so long, I was feeling a little uncertain about my role in this world.

But the truth is, I wanted to be noticed. I wanted to be admired. I wanted to feel important, relevant, and esteemed. Let me just call it what it is, pride – and not the good kind. It was the kind focused on self-promotion. And get this, that's what motivated Lucifer's rebellion against God and ultimately is at the root of all evil. Yuck!

Look, I believe the desires all of us have for significance and to be valued are God-given. And he intends to fulfill them within the embrace of his relationship with us. But pride's another thing altogether. It can never be satisfied. And the more you feed it, the more its hunger grows.

Jesus understood this and refused to allow himself to be in a position where he could even be tempted by it. He was leading us by example. Matthew's gospel says he withdrew from the spotlight at this moment of ecstatic popularity specifically to be alone with his Father in prayer.

And when we find ourselves in the crosshairs of the spirit of pride, we would be wise to do the same – turn and run to the throne of God. There's something about being on our knees before the Sovereign of the Universe that puts things in perspective and escorts us into a deep place of security that pride can't touch.

I'm writing this after having spent time at the Lord's feet regarding my sin described earlier. And as always, I discovered there his lavish grace to cover and cleanse. But I wonder, do you find yourself being offered pride's empty promises today? If so, don't hesitate. Run to the Father right now.

6:16-21 • Divine Guidance

Then they willingly received Him into the boat, and immediately the boat was at the land where they were going.
John 6:21

A fter Jesus fed the multitudes and withdrew from the crowds to be alone in prayer, a series of things took place that when you include the additional information supplied by the Gospels of Matthew and Mark illustrate important principles for anyone desiring divine guidance.

It was around sunset, and Jesus told the disciples to get into a boat and sail in the direction of the town of Capernaum – which wasn't very far away – along the north shore of the Sea of Galilee. And at first, they probably just hugged the coastline assuming Jesus would catch up to them on foot. But by nightfall, they still hadn't seen him, and a powerful storm came up which they battled all night while it forced them more than three miles out into the middle of the lake.

But we're told that Jesus was watching them the whole time. And suddenly, when it seemed things couldn't get any worse, there he was, drawing near to them – walking on the wind-whipped waves – assuring them everything would be OK as he got into the boat with them. Immediately after that, the storm miraculously ceased, and they found themselves at the "land where they were going."

Only…it wasn't Capernaum. It was Gennesaret.

Why the storm? Why the change in destination? Well, let's talk about it.

Most of us deeply desire to live our lives in obedience to God's will. We want to follow the path he's laid out for us. But much of the time we struggle to know what that is primarily because we're looking for the wrong things.

We're looking for a route that takes us along the path of least resistance. We don't want to face any obstacles, uphill climbs, or bad weather. But those are often the very things God needs to lead us through in order for his will to be fulfilled in our lives. The value of the personal and spiritual growth that results is priceless.

We also want to know where the road will take us before agreeing to set out on the journey. But it doesn't work that way. God's will is based on his eternal perspective, knowledge, and wisdom which are so infinitely higher than our own, we don't even have the frame of reference to comprehend that information. And if we could, we'd be tempted to plot our own course and leave him out of the picture altogether.

This brings me to the more important point. With God, it's all about the journey not the destination. The relationship, dependence, and faith we develop along the way are his priorities.

Here are some things to consider regarding divine guidance:

1. In the same way that Jesus sent the disciples in the direction of Capernaum but eventually brought them to Gennesaret, his guidance almost always begins with less clarity about the ultimate destination than you want. God can usually only give us enough of a glimpse to get us pointed in the right direction. But that's really all we need, because…

2. What's important is that we just keep putting one foot in front of the other, taking one step or one oar stroke at a time. Remember, it's all about the journey. And…

3. Don't panic or lose heart when a storm comes up and wonder why Jesus doesn't seem to be coming to your rescue. Just as he saw the disciples in the darkness, his

eye is on you too. And he will make his presence known, stepping into your boat right on time, stilling the storm, and delivering you safely to shore.

6:22-27 • Free Food

...You seek Me, not because you saw the signs, but because you ate of the loaves and were filled.

John 6:26b

These verses quietly cut like a knife to the heart of an issue I regularly need to reconsider. They challenge me to honestly evaluate why I follow Jesus.

After their hunger had been satisfied by the miracle of the loaves and fish, the crowds saw the disciples get into their only boat and depart. But they also noted that Jesus didn't go with them and headed off alone to a secluded area instead. Then, the next day, when they couldn't find him, they got into some other boats that had arrived later and went looking. When they located him, they wanted to know how he'd managed to get there.

He didn't tell them the dramatic story of how he'd walked on water. He chose instead to answer their question with a searing statement – one that revealed the true nature of why they'd followed him there.

To paraphrase, he said their pursuit was not because they'd just seen an amazing sign of his messiahship and wanted to submit to him as their Lord. He bluntly declared that the only reason they'd come looking for him was because he'd provided them with free food. Ouch!

He challenged them to stop viewing their relationship with him as a means of satisfying the temporary needs of the flesh, and to focus on eternity instead.

I have a relationship with the giant online retailer, Amazon. I pay an annual fee for its Prime membership so I can purchase items at what I hope will be discounted prices and have them shipped to me for free within two days. But that's as far as the relationship goes. It's transactional, and I'm at the center of it. I will pay that fee and be a loyal customer right up until the moment another company provides me with better prices or service. And if I'm honest, my relationship with Jesus can sometimes look like that.

I can sometimes drift into a state where I'm following him because of what he provides me – forgiveness of sins (1 John 1:9), peace that passes understanding (Philippians 4:7), joy inexpressible (1 Peter 1:8), the comfort of the Holy Spirit (Acts 9:31), and the supply of all my needs "according to his riches in glory" (Philippians 4:19). And as much as the Bible makes it abundantly clear he delights to bless me – and you – in these ways, Matthew 6:33 reminds us that it's after seeking him and his kingdom first that all these things are added to us. He wants a relationship with us that's anchored in the eternal not the temporal. He wants to lead us beyond the here and now into the forever after.

Lord, I pray you'd help me reclaim an eternal perspective as the only motive for why I follow you. May it always be that our relationship is centered around you alone.

6:28-29 • Scoot Over

This is the work of God, that you believe in Him whom He sent.
John 6:29b

Jesus told the crowds to spend their labor on that which is eternal not temporary, and they responded by asking him to explain. They wanted to know – as most people do – what kind of works please God.

But Jesus answered them in a completely unexpected way. Instead of telling them to pray, read the Bible, attend church, evangelize, tithe, love enemies, and feed the poor – along with a hundred other things we might have expected him to say – he told them that believing in him is the *doing* God is looking for from us.

When we hear this, most of us can't help but think there's got to be more to it. That's just too easy. Surely, pleasing God requires something more labor-intensive than that. Belief is just too simple.

But hold on, just because something is simple doesn't mean it isn't challenging. Climbing a mountain isn't complicated but it's also not easy. Placing my faith in Jesus is pretty straightforward but living it out requires everything I've got. Trusting him means placing my life, my future, my security, my provision – all that I am – in his hands.

And that's why verse 29 makes a lot of us uncomfortable. We'd prefer a list – no matter how long and complex – of things we need to *do* to please God because checking off a to-do list doesn't require surrendering control. Belief does.

So, we tend to want to add layers of *doing* to our relationship with God. It makes us feel like we're in the driver's seat. But it also leads to spiritual exhaustion because our sin has made it impossible to ever *do* enough.

So, let's keep it simple. Let's just scoot over to the passenger side and give him the wheel. Let's give up our *doing* and rest in what he's *done.*

6:30-36 • A Dog on a Bone

But I said to you that you have seen Me and yet do not believe.
John 6:36

Have you noticed how spiritually blind we can be when we become fixated on something we want?

Jesus told the people that believing in him as Messiah is the one thing God is asking us to do. And to paraphrase, they responded by saying, "If you really want us to believe that you're the Son of God, what miracle will you perform to convince us? Yes, we enjoyed the free meal you provided us the other day. But you only fed thousands and just once. Moses gave manna – the bread from heaven – to more than a million Israelites every day for forty years."

Jesus corrected them by clarifying that it wasn't Moses but God the Father who provided the manna during the wilderness wonderings and that it was meant to symbolize his ultimate provision of his Son to give life to the world.

Their reply sounds good: "Lord give us this bread always." But it's clear by the Lord's immediate response as well as what follows in the rest of the chapter that they still didn't get it. He bluntly stated, "I am the bread of life." And he went on to say that anyone who would come to him could have their spiritual hunger and thirst completely satisfied. Then he sadly added, "And yet you do not believe."

They were like a *dog on a bone*. They just could not let go of the dream of having Jesus provide them with free food. But their insistence on the satisfying of that desire caused them to miss the bigger picture altogether. And I'll bet you've experienced that yourself. I certainly have.

In fact, just a couple of weeks ago, I became infatuated with the idea of getting a pair of hiking boots like the ones I bought on our honeymoon when I was nineteen. I know it sounds crazy, but for several days I spent all my free time dreaming about how much better my life would be if could just relive that part of my wardrobe history. And after several internet searches, I actually found some for sale. I came remarkably close to spending $150 plus shipping on a pair of 44-year-old, used boots. Now, that's nuts!

What did I miss of my Savior's voice and the ministry of his Spirit during those days when I was so preoccupied with fulfilling my silly fantasy? What spiritual hungers went unsatisfied by the bread from heaven while I pursued that temporary satisfaction?

The same thing can happen when we get it in our heads that God ought to do what we think he should, when we think he should, and in the way we think he should. That presumption, if not quickly repented of, can grow to the point where it chokes off our spiritual sensitivities.

Be careful not to let that happen. Is there any desire that you're consumed with or insisting on today? Is the white-knuckled grip you have on that desire flowing out of your relationship with Jesus or something else? I encourage you to be honest with yourself and willing to surrender that hunger to him.

6:37-40 • Daily Believing Involves Daily Seeing

And this is the will of Him who sent Me, that everyone who sees the Son and believes in Him may have everlasting life...

John 6:40a

This part of the chapter is one of the hotspots in the predestination/freewill discussion that people much wiser and devoted than I am have gone back and forth about for centuries. And, although I have a deeply held opinion about this issue, I'm certain that nothing I have to say will change anyone's mind. So, I want to be upfront with the fact that I'm just not going to address that aspect of this passage.

Instead, I'd like to talk about the fact that there's more than one way to see something. For example, when I open my eyes and view the things in my field of vision, I'm seeing them. But if I take it a step further and carefully consider what my eyes have observed, it often results in an awareness or understanding that can also be described as seeing. I can see a painting hanging on a wall. But as I consider its artistic significance, I can come to see its depth, beauty, meaning, and importance. And I'm raising this distinction because it helps illuminate an important truth contained in this passage.

In verse 36, Jesus addressed the crowd that personally witnessed his power when he fed them by multiplying the loaves and fish. He said they'd *seen* him but did not believe. But, in verse 40, he said that everyone who *sees* him and believes will have everlasting life.

These two verses use two different Greek words to describe two different ways of seeing, resulting in two very different outcomes.

In English we have a saying, "Seeing is believing." But according to Jesus here, that's not always true. For instance, I think you'd agree that it's entirely possible for someone to see evidence of the power of God and still make the choice to not believe.

But since you've taken the time to read this today, it's likely you've seen and do believe. You've observed the display of God's power hanging in the gallery of the natural world, considered the exquisite truth depicted in his word, contemplated the gorgeous image of his grace portrayed in the cross, and as a result have chosen to place your faith in him as Savior.

But that seeing and believing is not just a one-time event. The Bible says in several places that we who have been justified by our faith in Jesus *live* by that faith (Habakkuk 2:4; Romans 1:17). Our believing is a daily thing. And I would suggest to you that daily believing involves daily seeing. Just because I've already chosen to believe doesn't mean I can afford to allow myself to stop carefully observing, considering, responding to, and delighting in the experiences of the revelation of the Lord on view moment-by-moment.

I want to see him today. How about you?

6:41-42 • The Issue of Familiarity

Is not this Jesus, the son of Joseph, whose father and mother we know?
How is it then that He says, "I have come down from heaven?"
John 6:42b

E arlier in the chapter, Jesus had announced to the crowd
that he was the bread of life sent from God to satisfy their
spiritual hunger. But now, in verses 41 and 42, we're told that
they — especially the religious elite who are described as *the Jews*
— were choking on this truth and unable to receive it because of
what they thought they knew about Jesus. They thought they
knew where he came from.

They knew he was raised in Joseph and Mary's household.
So, they just could not accept it when he claimed God was his
Father. Their familiarity with Jesus hindered them from hearing
what he said about himself — a truth they desperately needed to
embrace.

We all face a withering assault from the devil attempting to
keep us from the spiritual fulfillment God has provided in his
Son. And he does this by trying to convince us we are unloved,
forsaken, and forgotten. If he can't undo our salvation, he
intends to at least diminish its impact on our lives by attempting
to distort the truth about all Jesus is for us. Satan wants to keep
us bound in lives of frustration, discouragement, depression,
dishonor, and destruction.

But the truth sets us free (John 8:32). When we believe what
our Savior declares is true about himself and his love for us,
chains shatter, strongholds break. I've witnessed this miraculous
transformation in people's lives countless times over the years
of my pastoral ministry. And I've experienced it myself.

I've also noticed that one of the greatest challenges to being
able to hear Jesus when he speaks truth over us is familiarity —

that sense that we already know *where he's coming from*, so to speak. What we think we know *about* him can get in the way of our knowing who he really is.

This morning, I was trying to connect a device to my phone via Bluetooth. I know my way around digital gear, but I just couldn't get it to work. I was just about to go buy a new one when I decided to try once more. But this time, I followed the instructions in the owner's manual, and everything worked perfectly. I came very close to allowing my familiarity with technology to keep me from discovering something I needed to know to be able to benefit from that device.

I think you can tell where I'm going with this. Is there an area of your life that's just not working? If so, don't allow your familiarity with where you think the Lord is coming from regarding it keep you from receiving the important instructions in the owner's manual – the Bible – about who he is and wants to be for you. It's that truth about himself that will fix whatever's broken.

Lay the problem before him. Open his word. Quiet your heart. Hear his voice. Let his truth do its work.

6:43-44 • It's All Him

No one can come to Me unless the Father who sent Me draws him...
John 6:44a

J esus responded to the faithless murmurings of the Jewish religious elite regarding his claim of divinity by saying that embracing this truth is a response to something God initiates. It starts with him, not us. The process that results in placing faith in Christ begins with God drawing us toward belief.

There's something wonderful about that, don't you think? The realization that my faith in Jesus as Savior began with the Heavenly Father pursuing me, takes my breath away. I am his child because he wanted me. And if that weren't amazing enough, Jesus went on to say that my relationship with him will endure through the last day of my life in this world, and then, he will raise me up into his eternal presence.

And that reminds me of something.

Our youngest grandchildren are one-year-old twin girls. And the other day, I was watching one of them playing on the floor. I called out her name. And when she turned to look at me, I reached out to her, and she started crawling toward me. I gathered her up in my arms, snuggled her, kissed her cheek, told her I loved her, and would have held her like that all day if I could.

I know it's an imperfect example, but a relationship with Jesus is like that. It's all him not us. It's not about us finding him or trying desperately to hold on to him once we do. He reaches out to us. And then, when we respond to his great love, he wraps us in his embrace and holds on forever.

Rest in his love today. He desires you. He's holding on to you. And no matter what, he won't let go.

6:45-46 • Keys on the Ring

It is written in the prophets, "And they shall all be taught by God."
John 45:a

I love it when Jesus quotes Scripture! And that's what happened here. The Word of God was quoting the word of God. It's just so cool!

And he uses an interesting communication technique – one he employs in other places in the Gospels as well. He quotes just the first part of Isaiah 54:13 confident that it's so familiar his hearers will automatically recall the rest of the text.

It's like what happened the other day when a friend commented on the tendency of people to associate with others who share similar interests. My friend said, "Birds of a feather…" And he didn't have to finish the saying because he knew my mind would search my memory and fill in the rest, "…flock together." I knew the whole quote, "Birds of a feather flock together."

This technique stimulates a person to think more deeply about what's being said, and that's what Jesus wanted.

As his audience continued wrestling with his claim to be the bread of life, he wanted to lead them beyond the shallow, literal thinking that was constraining their ability to hear what he was really saying. So, he injected into the conversation a small piece of a very familiar and much-loved passage of Scripture that at first glance seems completely unrelated. But as their minds reflexively became engaged in the process of completing the quote, he knew they would find themselves recalling the sweet promises of God's grace contained in those verses.

He wanted them to see his role as bread of life in the context of that flow of God's redeeming love to them.

It's amazing how God's word can do that – take us to a

deeper and richer place when we get stuck on the surface. And that's part of the reason why it's so important to read the Bible and allow its treasures to become stored in our memories. It gives the Lord something to draw on when he needs to point our minds and hearts toward an unexpected discovery.

The direction of my entire adult life hinges on one of those times.

As a young man in my early twenties, I'd reached a point where my future was completely uncertain. It seemed that the trail I'd been following suddenly disappeared. My heart began to fill with anxiety and my mind became exhausted from running what-if scenarios.

Then, out of the blue, as I sat alone on a lunch break at my warehouse job, the first part of 2 Timothy 2:15 bubbled up unbidden into my thoughts from the place in my memory where I'd stored that verse as a child. And as my mind filled in the balance of the quote, I knew God was speaking to me through it. He was restoring a calling to pastoral ministry I thought I'd disqualified myself from, and he was preparing me for the next steps along that journey.

The door to the rest of my life opened in that moment and having that Bible verse committed to memory was the key.

I want to have lots of Scripture keys available to the Spirit when he desires to unlock things in my life, and I'll bet you do too. So, let's make a fresh commitment to having more keys on the ring by soaking in God's word today.

6:47-51 • You Are What You Eat

*I am the living bread which came down from heaven. If anyone eats of
this bread, he will live forever...*
John 6:51a

I'm a bottom-line kind of guy. As an internal processor, I
respond best to conversations when I know what we're
talking about upfront rather than having to wade through a
lengthy preamble or setup before arriving at the heart of the
matter.

God bless my dear wife. She's the exact opposite. She's a
verbal processor. Her most natural way to communicate is to
begin with a detailed description of the process that produced
what she wants to say before she actually says it.

Early in our marriage, this drove me crazy. But over the
years, I've come to appreciate and even highly value this aspect
of who she is. I've learned how to stay engaged with her
through these verbal wanderings and to even encourage them
because my life is vastly richer and my understanding much
broader due to this gift of her communication style.

But on those rare occasions when she approaches me with
the words, "Honey, here's the bottom line," I just go weak in
the knees, and I'm putty in her hands.

So, John 6:47 is my kind of verse.

With absolute clarity and economy of words, Jesus
emphatically stated the bottom line. He said, "He who believes
in me has everlasting life." Then, after coming right to the
point, he proceeded to explain what this kind of belief is like.

In verses 48 through 51, he described himself as the bread of
life and said that salvation is the result of eating this bread. And
he leaves no mystery about it. He plainly states that the bread
he's talking about is his body and that he will be offering it up in

order to provide life to the world.

In other words, saving faith requires more than just arriving at an intellectual or philosophical agreement with the truth of his saving grace. It requires consuming, taking in, or internalizing it. It means welcoming Jesus into our lives.

There's a saying, "You are what you eat." And it means the food we consume exerts profound influence on our lives. Our health, energy, appearance, mood, intelligence, and so much more are shaped by it. We literally can't live without it. But it has to be eaten in order to be of benefit. Being in the same room as a plate of food or just sitting there looking at it and considering its attributes will accomplish nothing.

In a similar way, exercising a faith that goes beyond mere contemplation and actually begins ingesting the bread of life is what brings our spirits to life and shapes every aspect of our eternal selves. So, you'll understand what I mean when I say salvation requires feasting on Jesus.

And he clarified what he meant by this when in Matthew 4:4 he quoted Moses in Deuteronomy 8:3 and said, "Man shall not live by bread alone, but by every word that proceeds from the mouth of God."

We internalize Jesus as we feed on God's word, the Bible. So today, let's sit down at the table he's prepared for us and dive in. Open his word and enjoy the feast that produces life everlasting.

6:52-59 • The Bridge Builder

These things He said in the synagogue as He taught in Capernaum.
John 6:59

This section closes the conversation Jesus had with the Jews about him being the true bread from heaven and the bread of life. This final passage begins by describing the struggle they had comprehending the concept of eating his flesh, or in other words, spiritually feasting on Jesus in order to gain eternal life.

But, without even a hint of frustration, the Lord patiently explained it all again, providing them with yet another opportunity to grasp this truth. He was building a bridge of understanding from something they already knew – manna in the wilderness – to something they didn't yet know – the cross. And even though we'll discover that most of them chose not to travel the span, this demonstration of his patient willingness to escort them over is deeply moving to me.

Why? Because I'm often very slow to comprehend spiritual truth. And knowing that my Savior won't give up on me and is willing to lovingly work with me until I get it is profoundly soul-securing.

For example, after forty-five years of marriage, I finally feel like I'm starting to understand what Ephesians 5:25 means when it says, "Husbands, love your wives, just as Christ loves the church and gave himself for her." And I can't thank Jesus enough for hanging in there with me through that steep learning curve because the impact on the sweetness of my relationship with Sue is simply indescribable.

We don't know what we don't know. So, in our human pride we assume we understand eternal things when we really don't. The truth is that our earth-bound, sin-scarred, and materialistic frame of reference is so narrow and shallow that we are completely dependent on the Bridge Builder to lead us from ignorance to knowledge. So, thank God we have the promise of John 16:13 – "He will guide you into all truth."

In light of the immeasurable kindness of our patient, loving teacher, let's stay teachable today as he leads us from what we think we know to what we have yet to discover.

6:60-66 • The Ecstasy of Access

And He said, "Therefore I have said to you that no one can come to
Me unless it has been granted to him by My Father."
John 6:65

In these verses, we encounter a sad fact and a breathtaking reality.

The sad fact is that some people will make the choice to turn away from following Jesus.

The passage opens by disclosing that many of those who'd been following him since the loaves and fish miracle and heard him describe himself as the bread from heaven that provides eternal life, complained that they just couldn't understand his message. They said it was too hard to grasp.

He responded by saying that if they couldn't comprehend this prerequisite truth, they would certainly not be able to move on to the rest of what could be revealed to them. He also clarified the problem as a paradigm issue not a communication failure. It was neither that they weren't intelligent enough nor that he wasn't clear. It was that they were refusing to let go of their faithless frame of reference.

A paradigm is a framework of understanding. It's the lens we see things through. And when he said, "The flesh profits nothing," he meant that insisting their humanistic, natural-world, unbelieving framework could handle spiritual understanding was folly. He was introducing them to a whole new paradigm. He wasn't just trying to get a point across, his words were literally spirit and life.

He went on to say their comprehension problem was not the difficulty of the concepts, it was their lack of faith. Belief is the first step into the paradigm of the spirit, and it cannot be skipped. As long as a person resists believing in Christ, there's only so much they can receive from him. And sadly, many in this crowd had reached the end of the line. So, they walked away.

But not all of them. And that's where we discover the breathtaking reality described in the heart of verse 65.

Here we see a completely different outcome for those of us who do choose to believe. Instead of turning away, we find ourselves coming to Jesus. And we're told the Heavenly Father is the one who grants this amazing access.

This is stunning on so many levels. It means that when we're hurting, we can come to Jesus. When we're weak, we can come to Jesus. And it also means when we're confused, unclear, or uncertain about anything, we can come to Jesus.

So even though we might encounter spiritual truths that initially challenge our comprehension, our faith has ushered us into the paradigm of the Spirit and given us direct access to the one who can and will open those truths to us.

I challenge you. Don't be among those who turn away in unbelief. Daily choose to faithfully, fearlessly, and continuously follow Jesus by faith and experience the ecstasy of access.

6:67-71 • Believe and Know

...We have come to believe and know that You are the Christ, the Son of the living God.
John 6:69b

The sixth chapter of John's Gospel concludes with a soaring declaration of faith along with a sobering reminder.

In verse 67, Jesus turned his attention from the many to the few. For most of this chapter, Jesus was focused on the multitude. He had compassionately and skillfully revealed himself to them and led them to a decision point regarding his messiahship. But when they reached that point, sadly, most of them chose to remain in their unbelief and walked way.

Then, as the crowd was deserting him, he turned and confronted the twelve. He asked if they were going to abandon him as well. Peter's response was literally one for the ages. He said, "Lord, to whom shall we go? You have the words of eternal life." And then he said, "We have come to *believe* and *know* that you are the Christ, the Son of the Living God."

His statements are so powerful! And I'd like to draw your attention to his use of two specific words: *believe* and *know*. With them he articulated the breadth of what it means to have faith in Christ. The Greek word translated as *believe* is *pisteuo*, and it describes a belief that chooses to commit. The other word, *know*, is translated from the word *ginosko*, and it refers to a knowledge that is more experiential than intellectual.

The faith Peter described is the result of both a choice and an experience, a decision and a relationship. We can't have one without the other and we can't reverse the order. Without choosing to commit, there can't be an experience. And a decision to believe that doesn't result in a relationship is incomplete.

True faith is like a marriage. It begins with a choice to commit, but unless that decision results in a relational experience, something's seriously wrong.

And that's why on the heels of Peter's soaring statement that he assumed was true for all of them, Jesus' next question is a sobering reminder. In a sense he used the question to say, "Peter, the faith you've so eloquently defined is not true for all of you." And we're told he was referring to Judas, who would eventually betray him.

It's not possible to know exactly what was insufficient with Judas' believing that allowed for his betrayal. But it's clear that he'd made some kind of commitment to follow Jesus. That's why he was there that day counted among the disciples. My hunch is that something was deficient in his pursuit of an experience with the Lord.

May that not be true of you and me. Let's invite the Holy Spirit to reveal and deal with anything about our faith that looks like a commitment without a relationship. Let's daily choose to pursue the one who has invited us into a belief that results in an experience.

The John Project

ACKNOWLEDGMENTS

I'd like to thank all those who've watched, "liked," and commented on the John Project videos over the last few years. Your accompaniment and encouragement along this journey kept me going and gave me the confidence to stare down my fear of the blank page and start the writing that became this book.

I also want to express my gratitude to those who offered the immeasurable gifts of their time, skill, intelligence, and talent to help me improve my writing and make his book better. Rachel Lobo, Barney Wiget, Eric Jensen, Steve Steffy, and Amy Stevens challenged me to focus more, think deeper, and work harder. I am richly blessed to have them in my life.

ABOUT THE AUTHOR

Randy Boldt served for nearly forty years as a local church pastor and regional overseer for his denomination before launching Crosspointe Ministries along with his wife, Sue, in 2018. Crosspointe is now the platform they use for strengthening married couples through their Regal Romance events, helping people experience healing from wounds to their souls through their Steps to Breakthrough conferences, providing pastoral care to students and staff working with Youth With A Mission (YWAM) in the nation of Taiwan, mentoring young pastors and church leaders, and creating Bible teaching content.

The Boldts have been married for 45 years and love, love, love their family which includes three adult children and their spouses along with a total of seven grandchildren. They make their home in Southern California.

You can find more of Randy's teaching (audio, video, & text), at randyboldt.com.

65429066R00106

Made in the USA
Middletown, DE
05 September 2019